The Twitter Workbook

The Twitter Workbook

by David R Haslam

HMSI Publications
Plymouth, Michigan
U.S.A.

www.HMSI-inc.com

The Twitter Workbook

@TTWB on Twitter.com

Published by HMSI Publications, a division of HMSI, inc. www.HMSI-inc.com
Authored by David R Haslam, @DavidRHaslam
Copy Editing by Beverly Cornell, @beverlycornell
Technical Editing by Danielle Zhu, @dzhu
Internet Marketing by Lori Martin Harris, @LoriMHarris
Cover Art by Elena Covalciuc, @EleART

Proofreaders: Patricia Berkopec, Drita Dokic, Mayna Schumacher, Monica Tombers, and The Haslams

TRADEMARKS: The author has attempted in this book to indicate where proprietary trademarks are used. To distinguish them from descriptive terms, the manufacturer's capitalization has been used.

SOFTWARE: The author and publisher have made their best efforts to use the currently released versions of software during the preparation of this book. Further, the author and publisher make no representation or warranties of any kind with regard to the accuracy or completeness of the contents herein and accept no liability of any kind including but not limited to performance, merchantability, fitness for any particular purpose, or any losses or damages of any kind caused or alleged to be caused directly or indirectly from this book.

SERVICES: The author and publisher are not engaged in rendering legal, accounting, marketing, or any other professional services solely by the purchase of this book. If expert assistance is needed, please seek the services of a competent professional.

CONTACT: The author and publisher have attempted to contact all entities discussed in any detail in this book. This includes but is not limited to any individual who was referenced during an interview or descriptive text.

Most of the quotations used for Part, Chapter, and Case Study title pages where found on http://thinkexist.com The author wishes thank the community for its collection. Other quotations used are referenced according to the source.

ISBN – 10: 0-615-29442-1
ISBN – 13: 978-0-61529442-1

Designed, developed, and printed in the United States of America

10 9 8 7 6 5 4 3 2 1

Past:
To my grandparents

Present:
To Cecilia and my children

Future:
To my grandchildren

Acknowledgements

"Knowledge is in the end based on acknowledgement"
— *Ludwig Wittgenstein*

Where to begin? So many people I am grateful to. First of all, I would like to praise God for keeping me strong, healthy, and focused through this process.

Next, I would like to thank EVERYONE named in this book. Without your contribution to the text, this book could not have been created! For a full listing, see www.hmsi-inc.com/ttwb .

In addition, I want to thank the three people that gave me the specific inspiration to even think about writing this. Danielle Zhu for introducing me to a dynamic, exciting, can-do group of people that are at the core of this book. Jackie Silver pointed me in the direction of how to get it printed and distributed, and make it worthwhile financially. And finally, Dr. Ann Burton, who one misty winter's morning said to me, "Why don't you write a book on how to use Twitter!" Thank you for the idea Dr B.

Thank you to my "staff" ☺. Pat, Drita, Mayna, and Monica for the many hours you spent proof reading this and beating it into shape. Danielle and Beverly for the boundless support, energy, and ideas while editing the book. Lori for applying your marketing knowledge and enthusiasm to the project. Elena for your creativity and patience with me in designing the covers, and your many hours of support via chat, e-mail, and of course Twitter. I'm looking forward to speaking to you AND meeting you in person.

I'm eternally grateful to my long term support systems. These are the groups and people who have shown faith in my abilities when others walked away. They include the members of Dearborn Dynamic and Tier One Talkers Toastmasters, Rotary Club of Plymouth a.m., the InSights Group, and St. John's Episcopal Church, Plymouth. Also Jim and Ray, Dorian, Peter, and Paul, Kate, Deb and Dawn (good luck in Texas, we'll miss you!), Nancy, Kevin, and Robynn, Dani, Mike, Ruth, and Ali. Without you, this would not have happened.

And my final thank you is to my entire long suffering family. My four sisters, their husbands, and children. My adopted family, The Wilkins. My Jason and Deanna and their families. But most especially Matt and Cecilia who have had to put up with me on a daily basis. All the best at Central Michigan next year Matt! I'll miss your field trips and late night conversations about EVERYTHING! And honey, we finally have some time alone ☺.

Thank you, and I love you all!

David R. Haslam
Plymouth, Michigan
June, 2009

P.S. Thanks for the lunch Kristan! I told you I'd do it!!

The Twitter Workbook

"The Chinese use two brush strokes to write the word 'crisis'. One brush stroke stands for danger; the other for opportunity. In a crisis, be aware of the danger – but recognize the opportunity."
- Richard M. Nixon

Introduction

"Fear not that thy life shall end, but rather fear that it shall never have a beginning"
    – *John Henry Cardinal Newman*

Twitter is currently THE fastest growing online social network. From February 2008 to February 2009, the user community increased by 1,382% according to Nielsen. And the growth is continuing.

Before you take the plunge and join the Twitter revolution there are three questions you may have:

- First, why should you use Twitter?
- Second, how do you use it?
- Third who is using it for what?

'The Twitter Workbook' is divided into five parts to deal with those three questions:

- Part 1 is 'Beginning with Twitter' which briefly explains why and how to use Twitter. If you want to get going as quickly as possible, Part 1 is for you!
- Part 2 is 'Why use Twitter?' This describes in greater depth why you should join the Twitterverse and things to consider before and after you get started.

- Part 3 is 'How to Twitter?' It contains a more detailed account of how to use Twitter and how to make the most of the service.
- Part 4 is 'Who uses Twitter?' This short section gives information on some great <u>Tweeps</u>. It's designed to give you ideas of why people are using Twitter and what types of business they are in.
- Part 5 *is actually spread throughout the book.* It's a series of case studies and interviews from a variety of people who have had success with Twitter. The case studies should help you decide the Twitter strategies you will use to meet your goals.

1. A Few Definitions

Let's take a look at a few definitions from www.Dictionary.com :

so·cial ◁) [soh-shuhl] [?] Show IPA

–adjective

1. pertaining to, devoted to, or characterized by friendly companionship or relations: *a social club.*
2. seeking or enjoying the companionship of others; friendly; sociable; gregarious.
3. of, pertaining to, connected with, or suited to polite or fashionable society: *a social event.*
4. living or disposed to live in companionship with others or in a community, rather than in isolation: *People are social beings.*
5. of or pertaining to human society, esp. as a body divided into classes according to status: *social rank.*
6. involved in many social activities: *We're so busy working, we have to be a little less social now.*
7. of or pertaining to the life, welfare, and relations of human beings in a community: *social problems.*
8. noting or pertaining to activities designed to remedy or alleviate certain unfavorable conditions of life in a community, esp. among the poor.
9. pertaining to or advocating socialism.
10. *Zoology.* living habitually together in communities, as bees or ants. Compare SOLITARY (def. 8).
11. *Botany.* growing in patches or clumps.
12. *Rare.* occurring or taking place between allies or confederates.

Perhaps any one of the first four could be used for social media or networking. But we will choose number one: "pertaining to, devoted to, or characterized by friendly companionship or relations"

me·di·a[1] ◁)) [mee-dee-*uh*] [?] Show IPA

–noun
1. a pl. of MEDIUM.
2. (*usually used with a plural verb*) the means of communication, as radio and television, newspapers, and magazines, that reach or influence people widely: *The media are covering the speech tonight.*

–adjective
3. pertaining to or concerned with such means: *a job in media research.*

Usage note:
MEDIA, like *data*, is the plural form of a word borrowed directly from Latin. The singular, MEDIUM, early developed the meaning "an intervening agency, means, or instrument" and was first applied to newspapers two centuries ago. In the 1920s MEDIA began to appear as a singular collective noun, sometimes with the plural MEDIAS. This singular use is now common in the fields of mass communication and advertising, but it is not frequently found outside them: *The media is* (or *are*) *not antibusiness.*

Definition number two is appropriate: "the means of communication, as radio and television, newspapers, and magazines that reach or influence people widely".

Taken together as social media, a definition does not appear on the site. However, let us define it as "the information generated by the users of online social networks within those networks". For example when you create a Tweet using Twitter, the Tweet is social media, and Twitter is the social network.

net·work ◁)) [net-wurk] ? Show IPA

—noun

1. any netlike combination of filaments, lines, veins, passages, or the like: *a network of arteries; a network of sewers under the city.*
2. *Radio and Television.*
   a. a group of transmitting stations linked by wire or microwave relay so that the same program can be broadcast or telecast by all.
   b. a company or organization that provides programs to be broadcast over these stations: *She was hired by the network as program coordinator.*
3. a system of interrelated buildings, offices, stations, etc., esp. over a large area or throughout a country, territory, region, etc.: *a network of supply depots.*
4. *Electricity.* an arrangement of conducting elements, as resistors, capacitors, or inductors, connected by conducting wire.
5. a netting or net.
6. *Telecommunications, Computers.* a system containing any combination of computers, computer terminals, printers, audio or visual display devices, or telephones interconnected by telecommunication equipment or cables: used to transmit or receive information.
7. an association of individuals having a common interest, formed to provide mutual assistance, helpful information, or the like: *a network of recent college graduates.*

Definition number seven is clearly the best when applied to social networks. www.Dictionary.com defines a social network as:

social network - 3 dictionary results

Main Entry: social network[1]
Part of Speech: *n*
Definition: a person's family, neighbors, and friends with whom they are socially involved

Main Entry: social network[2]
Part of Speech: *n*
Definition: a website where one connects with those sharing personal or professional interests, place of origin, education at a particular school, etc.
Usage: computing

This book deals with the latter of the two definitions. However, a few times in conversation people have asked about the former. The original form of social network (family, neighbors, and friends) is still vitally important. Combining traditional (real life) social networks with the internet style is the best way of all to network.

2. My Twitter Story (Part 1)

My very first exposure to Twitter was in the cafeteria at the University of Colorado in Boulder, Colorado, during the summer of 2008. I was presenting to the 11th Mars Society Convention. At lunch on the first day my partners were David Jedynak and Tanya Luzan. We had been discussing the wonders of modern technology and advances in communication over our 'student style' lunches, when David mentioned Twitter. Tanya and I listened intently as he explained this new frontier of communication to us. He shared in basic terms how it worked and then told the story of a man in Egypt who had used Twitter to help in getting his release from jail. We were all hooked! David went on to explain more about the system, and what people were using it for at that time. Naturally, I did what most people do when they hear about something 'cool' for the first time. I moved my attention immediately to something else and forgot about it! In my case, the something else was Facebook, as that was all the rage at the convention as well.

On that same day my great friend at Crestview Technologies, Danielle Zhu, registered me up for a special event scheduled at Automation Alley, in Troy, Michigan in early September. Of all the amazing events that happened to me during 2008, that first Automation Alley event was probably the most significant. The event was the last of the big catalysts that altered my life last year...

Twitter has changed people's lives. It allows news to be spread farther, wider, and more quickly than any other media currently available. In November 2008, a US Marine Corps jet crashed in San Diego County in Southern California. I learned about the incident on Twitter BEFORE it was reported on the 24 hour news networks! It has become a primary source of news for many, including reporters!

Twitter has changed the way business is conducted. I have seen Twitter in action for arranging vacations, real estate transactions, training and education planning, event coordination, note taking at meetings, amateur sports reporting, political discussions, and a myriad of other uses. And of course, nerds, geeks, and savvy marketing people love it!

Twitter has changed how families and friends communicate. Arranging get-togethers (or Tweet-ups) on the fly, coordinating meetings whether formal or informal, letting others know about weather and traffic issues, and even telling others where to find great deals at a mall or online. The list of uses is endless! Unlike a telephone conversation, Twitter is permanent. Unlike a text message, Twitter can be accessed anywhere.

Twitter not only transmits the news, it IS the news! Almost all information delivery services, from traditional newspapers to modern web based blogs keep their followers informed via Twitter. And from the Hudson River plane crash to Obama's first State-of-the-Union speech, Twitter has been repeatedly commented on by its rival sources of instant news updates.

3. Updates and Registration

The purpose of this book is to educate and entertain. It is to help you get started with Twitter, and make the most of it when you enter the Twitterverse! If you have any questions, comments, suggestions, or just good stories to share, find me at www.Twitter.com/davidrhaslam, or send a message to @davidrhaslam on Twitter.

Between new releases of the book, we will put any updates on the HMSI Publications website. To access the updates, go to www.HMSI-inc.com/ttwb and follow the instructions to register your copy of the book.

And by the way, use the hash tag #TTWB in your correspondence. ☺ Don't know what I'm talking about? Read on...

Case Studies Introduction

"Our best thoughts come from others."
- *Ralph Waldo Emerson*

Why reinvent the wheel? The fastest way to move in a new direction is to learn from those that have gone before you. This requires three basic things to happen:

1. Find someone to learn from
2. See if they are willing to educate you
3. Make sure you are ready and willing to learn

At the end of each chapter the case studies explore different approaches to old challenges. Chosen to amuse, inspire, or amaze, all are there to learn from.

The Thirteen Answers!

A little caution for you, the intrepid reader! It is said that if you ask 12 engineers how to build something, you will get 13 answers, and so it was with the Tweeps in the case studies. Though they all had the same questions, they gave an array of sometimes contradictory answers. None the less it was fun to talk to with each of them.

Throughout the book, the case studies have this simple border. You can easily find them or skip them depending on your needs.

The case studies express the views and opinions of the people interviewed, and not necessarily those of the author or publisher. Please take the case studies as examples and not as sure fire success plans for Twitter.

Part 1 – Beginning with Twitter

"The first step towards getting somewhere is to decide that you are not going to stay where you are."

>   *- Unknown Author*

Chapter 1 - Is Twitter for you?

"Sometimes it's the smallest decisions that can change your life forever"
- *Ken Russell*

You are in control of your destiny! Only you can decide to Tweet or not. Nobody can force you to join Twitter. Let's take a look to see what it's all about.

1. What is Twitter?

Twitter is termed a 'micro-blog'. A weblog, usually called a blog, is a website where the owner can write text, display photographs and graphics, or show videos. Currently, there are over 150 million blogs worldwide. Blogs can vary in length, style, and content as much as the people who write them vary in age, outlook, and experience. Blogs are an established way of getting your message out to the rest of the internet.

With Twitter you are restricted to only 140 characters in a Tweet (as a Twitter message is called). However, those 140 characters can include links to other web addresses, and therefore can link to blogs, home pages, or any other type of web page. This is the power of Twitter. Simplicity, flexibility, and universality. It is changing how people communicate '*140 characters at a time*'.

2. My Twitter Story (Part 2)

I can vouch for the power of Twitter! I have found many contacts via Twitter that would have been more difficult, even impossible to reach otherwise. I have made thousands of dollars using it to market myself to people who can use my skills. I'm a speaker, trainer, and author. Each of those three realms has secured business through Twitter. My company, and affiliates, also create graphics, artwork, website design, and enterprise 2.0 solutions. They, too, have benefited directly from my involvement on Twitter. You see it's not all about me. In fact, good social networking should never be solely about you. You should always focus more attention on others than yourself. This is a wise investment with unexpected dividends.

A sample of the power of Twitter: take a look at the cover of this book. It was designed by Elena (@ElenART). As the first edition of this book goes to press, Elena and I have only used Twitter, along with the occasional e-mail, to communicate with each other. We have never met, and never even heard the sound of each others voice (unless she saw me on YouTube!) Elena and I worked very efficiently together and got the cover designed and approved within days. I'm in Michigan and she is in Florida. We both work from our home offices with no commuting. We have learned to work very flexibly, openly, and in a very trusting and cooperative way. It has been an absolute pleasure! Trusting and cooperating is what makes the human race great and social systems work. So it is with Twitter.

3. How people use Twitter

According to the website, www.Twitter.com, you use it to report "what you are doing". However, people would rapidly lose interest if all the Tweets were about brushing your teeth, drinking coffee, or leaving for work.

We are not all pop-culture stars, but more and more of them are adopting Twitter to keep their name talked about. The old saying 'there is no such thing as bad publicity' applies here. The growing trend in pop-culture is to spread the desired message through social media tools such as Twitter because spreading the message is what pop-culture is all about.

TV, radio, newspaper, magazine advertising, and even Internet ads can cost millions of dollars. Social media marketing is *very* low cost in comparison. If you are prepared to spend the time, and not count that as cost, it can be free!

Ask people who use Twitter (called Tweeps or Tweeple in the Twitterverse) what they Tweet about and you'll get an array of answers. Below is just a sample. You should use Twitter in the way that suits your individual style. Do not worry about changing what you do. Not withstanding life's regular consideration of morals, ethics, and consequences, there is no wrong or right thing to Tweet about.

- Personal use: What you are doing in your personal life that you care to share?
- Branding: Build brand awareness by Tweeting about activities and success stories.
- Event promotion: Keeping people informed about events and how to attend them.

- Product launch: Support activities concerned with the launch of a new product or service.
- Non-profit activity: To share ideas and ventures undertaken by non-profit organizations to increase participation.
- Meeting notes: Use to record and share ideas during meetings for you and your followers / group to use.
- Instant news: Report news as it happens. Possibly even help the people involved in the news.
- Event updates: Inform people of events as they take place *and if things change.*
- Weather and traffic reporting: Instant access to local information.
- Job postings: Post jobs for instant responses. (Especially used by savvy recruiters and managers.)
- Finding a job: Search for the latest jobs and respond quickly. (The mark of a savvy job hunter!)
- Ask questions: Get quick answers to your questions.
- Give good answers: Return the favor by answering questions, if you have the knowledge. Don't guess or give false information as it will affect your reputation.

You can stop using Twitter at anytime if you do not like it. You can also make your updates private and block other users from following you. (More about following later). If you do "go private", you have to approve each of your followers. This can reduce the possibility of strangers knowing too much about you.

Some people take a while to grasp the power of using Twitter, and this is OK. In fact, when you read the case studies, you'll find that most of the people featured took time to get used to Twitter. It is not uncommon to hear Tweeps say "I just didn't get it when I started". However the power of Twitter is there if you take the time to explore it. Give it some time, use it for fun, and keep at it. You never know what you might discover,

Write down any ideas that you may have for subjects to Tweet about. Be creative!:

_____

_____

_____

_____

_____

_____

_____

_____

_____

Case Study 1 – The Average Josephine?

"Normal is not something to aspire to, it's something to get away from."
 - *Jodie Foster*

In the Introduction to this book, I mentioned an event at Automation Alley in Troy, Michigan that took place in September, 2008. At the "Getting <u>LinkedIn</u>: Creating Business Connections!" event, which was the first time I ever visited 'The Alley', I met the incomparable Beverly Cornell, who was one of the star presenters.

Beverly, from Itero Text Translation Services, was talking about her first love in social networking software, LinkedIn. I learned so much about LinkedIn but what struck me most were the antics of the front row of people during the presentation. Instead of paying 'rapt attention' to the speaker, they were constantly tapping away on computers, Blackberries, and cell phones. At the time, I thought that was extremely rude! How wrong was I! You see, THIS was my first direct exposure to Twitter.

Dave Biskner (see Case Study 2), and Terry Bean (see Case Study 3) were the other two presenters. And, amongst many others in attendance were Kevin Krason and Shauna Nicholson (see Case Study 2 as well!). They were all involved in Tweeting during the meeting. Of course, I later found out having people Tweet your every word is in fact very complimentary in this day and age. Heck, the Congress and Senate now Tweet when the President speaks!

Beverly was one of the first half dozen people I began to follow on Twitter. I think it is appropriate to share her views on Twitter, as she helped educate me. Hopefully you can gain from her wisdom as well:

1). Twitter ID:
@BeverlyCornell

2). Personal or corporate use?
"Social media, and in particular Twitter, is an opportunity to represent yourself, as well as the brand you work for. Whatever your feelings are about your brand, positive or negative, it will reveal itself in Twitter. If you are excited about your job, or frustrated with it, your Tweets will reflect that. In that case it is a personal side of you and your business life. A combination of both!"

3). Did you try anything similar before Twitter?
"My social networking began with LinkedIn about four years ago. I then leaped into Facebook, started a blog, began podcasting, and only a year ago started twittering. It is official. I am a social networking addict and I am afraid if you are reading this case study that I may be contributing to your addiction as well."

4). Who introduced you to it?
"In the winter of 2008, I had been reading about Twitter and hearing some 'buzz,' but I didn't really dive into Twitter until I saw Chris Lakatos, President of Netpods (@netpods and @capitalbug) using it at an event. After a five minute conversation with Chris about Twitter, I went

home that night and setup my account. I started by listening."

5). When did you start?
"April 2008 is when I joined but I don't think I really understood the power of Twitter right away. I started with a lot of listening. It took about three months for me to feel comfortable participating and sharing my Tweets. I think I wanted to learn the rules of the road."

6). Why do you use Twitter?
"To be honest, initially I thought Twitter was just noise and was going to be a distraction. However, after a few months of listening, I realized Twitter is like a grand sociology experiment. You can see people talking about themselves, their lives, their work, and each other. You can learn and discuss major world, local, and personal events all in one location and in 140 characters or less! Brilliant!"

7). What do you Tweet about?
"I comment on other Tweets. I share re-Tweets that I find interesting. I recommend great articles. I talk about odd things I encounter during my day. I ask burning questions. I vent a frustration, or reveal something I'm excited about. Once in awhile I also Tweet about something new at work, a blog update and my podcast links. I make sure I Tweet a wide variety of subjects and that at least 90% of it is NOT about me telling or selling to my Tweeps."

8). Any advice that you would like to share?
"Twitter is about YOU and your personality. NEVER go for the hard sell. Keep it real and personal. Remember, you are at an online cocktail party, be a good conversationalist! The challenge I see with social media is that we tend to self select the information we follow. I see

people following other people just like them with their same perspectives. Be curious and check out people not from your neighborhood, not in your field of business and not in this country. See what the world is talking about. You never know what you might learn. You may create a friendship, or accidentally meet the best customer your business has ever had. Be open! Twitter is a great place to exchange ideas. Always share in the lively discussions occurring. In a way, it is like a water cooler conversation without the water cooler and the staff! Twittering is a great way for small business owners and home based workers to avoid feeling isolated."

9).   Your best Twitter experience?
        "Back in the fall of 2008, I was attending an event at Wayne State University (WSU) in Detroit. While at the event, I Twittered that I was at WSU to hear Vicente Fox, former President of Mexico, speak about globalization and immigration issues. In less than a minute, I received a reply from WSU thanking me for attending and that they looked forward to my Tweets about the event! I was so impressed by the level of attention that WSU was giving to their brand and who was talking about them. Sometime later, Business Week was asking for stories on how people had used Twitter. I shared my WSU experience, and the story was quoted on the front page of Business Week!"

10).   Top three Tweeps that you would recommend?
        @QueenofSpain
        @MCHammer
        @CindyKing

11).   Other social networks you use regularly?
        "LinkedIn (business focused), Facebook (personal focused), Motor City Connect (networking locally), Internations.org (networking globally)"

12).   What do you think your future with Twitter will be?
    "The opportunities are endless here. It is a powerful tool that can be used for networking, brand building, friendship creating, and general information gathering. What you put in – you will get out! "

Chapter 2 - Quick Start

"Make haste slowly"
  – *Benjamin Franklin*

These instructions assume no prior knowledge of Twitter. They are designed to get you started quickly.

If you want a more in depth look at setting up your Twitter account, go to Chapter 7. That chapter includes more information on choosing your e-mail account, user name, and a number of other things. This can be important if you are using Twitter for marketing and branding purposes.

If an area in this chapter is covered in more depth in Chapter 7, it is marked with "*". There is a lot of information that could affect your decisions before you start. However if you just want to get on with it, turn the page to start your adventure!

1). Make sure you have an e-mail account on which you do not mind getting SPAM. Not to accuse Twitter of spamming; it is just a good idea for virtual social networking in general.

E-mail Address:_____

2). Open your Internet browser of choice (Internet Explorer, Firefox, Opera, etc.)

3). Go to www.Twitter.com.

4). Click the 'Get Started – Join!' button at the lower center of the web page.

5).* Enter the full name as you would like it to appear on your profile.

Name:_____

Full name   **Twitt Workbook**   ✔ ok

6).* Enter your user name. (Letters and numbers only. No spaces or special characters).

User Name:_____

Username   **TwittWorkbook**   ✔ ok

7).* Enter your password.

Password:_____

Password   ••••••••••   ✔ Good

8). Enter your e-mail address (from Step 1).

Email twittbook@comcast.net ✅ ok

9). Click on the box if you want the inside scoop.

☐ I want the inside scoop—please send me email updates!

10).* Type in the "anti-bot" words shown on the screen.

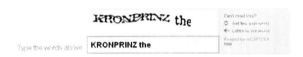

11). Click the "Create My Account" button.

Create my account

12).* The next screen is "See if your friends are on Twitter". Since this is quick start, click "Skip this step" at the bottom.

13).* The final screen is "Look who else is here…" These are famous / infamous Tweeps. (Click on any that you might be interested in). Click the "Finish" button.

14). Type in "Greetings! I'm finally on Twitter! #TTWB", and click "update". You have just sent your first Tweet!

Congratulations!!! You are now part of the Twitterverse!

Case Study 2 – The Tweet Company

"Normal is not something to aspire to, it's something to get away from."
  - *Jodie Foster*

'In-real-life' networking events, I love them! They are a chance to meet new people, find new ideas, and create new opportunities. I have already mentioned the "Getting LinkedIn: Creating Business Connections!" event. Along with Beverly Cornell (see Case Study 1), Dave Biskner, COO of Biznet and Terry Bean, co-founder of Motor City Connect presented their thoughts and advice on LinkedIn. Once the formal part of the meeting was over (and, as described in Case Study 1, the front row Tweeting had stopped), I was introduced to Dave.

Soft spoken, but always open and friendly, Dave treated me like a long lost friend. He proceeded to introduce me to the other members of Biznet at the meeting. These included Kevin Krason, the CEO, and Shauna Nicholson, the Marketing Manager.

From that first meeting, Biznet's grasp of social networking has impressed me. They have embraced these new communication tools and leading the charge in this realm is Shauna. A tall, slender, perpetually smiling young lady, she has a way of developing friendships from any situation. Well respected by her peers, she has demonstrated how to use Twitter to engage people and foster positive relationships. I think her story may truly inspire others to use the full capabilities of social networking.

My interview with Shauna was conducted using Skype. Skype is a great communication system (www.Skype.com) that enables audio and video on the web. At my request, we used the Skype chat feature to record the interview. The actual screen prints are shown.

David R Haslam says: 2:34:44 PM
Q1. What is your Twitter address?

Shauna Nicholson says: 2:34:52 PM
@shaunan

                                                              2:34:56 PM
or @shaunabiznet

David R Haslam says: 2:36:12 PM
Q2. Personal or Corporate use of Twitter?

Shauna Nicholson says: 2:36:21 PM
both

                                                              2:36:41 PM
Personal--Great to organize a meet up with friends, make new friends, and share ideas and opinions.

                                                              2:37:27 PM
Business-- Perfect for sharing resources with links and quick tips. I have an inspirational network, so they're always keeping me thinking of new ideas.

David R Haslam says: 2:37:57 PM
Great...

                                                              2:38:01 PM
Q3. Did you try anything similar or any other social media before Twitter?

Shauna Nicholson says: 2:39:04 PM
Similiar, no. I've had a Facebook since it was a college-only network.

                                                              2:39:12 PM
I had MySpace before, but never got too hooked on it.

                                                              2:39:22 PM
LinkedIn, of course.

2:39:35 PM

Oh, and a writers community

2:39:42 PM

I think that's it.

David R Haslam says: 2:39:57 PM

Good. 🙂

2:40:07 PM

So far so good...

2:40:09 PM

Q4. Who introduced Twitter to you?

Shauna Nicholson says: 2:40:56 PM

You know, I don't remember. It might have been Victoria (@typeis4lovers), because we joined on the same day.

David R Haslam says: 2:41:19 PM

OK

2:41:22 PM

Q5. When did you start using it?

Shauna Nicholson says: 2:41:48 PM

May 6, 2008

2:41:54 PM

http://whendidyoujointwitter.appspot.com/

2:41:55 PM

🙂

David R Haslam says: 2:42:11 PM

Nice! Love it!

2:42:24 PM

Q5. Why do you use it?

Shauna Nicholson says: 2:43:20 PM

It's a quick, unobtrusive way to share information; personal or for business. I love that I can TwitPic a quick shot of what I'm doing or simply post a link and headline.

   2:43:49 PM

I've built a lot of great professional relationships and friendships. In fact, Twitter networked my way to my position at Biznet.

David R Haslam says: 2:44:40 PM

OK. Hold that thought... That may be ideal for what is coming up...

Shauna Nicholson says: 2:45:06 PM

ok

David R Haslam says: 2:45:13 PM

Q7. What do you Tweet about?

Shauna Nicholson says: 2:46:30 PM

Hm

David R Haslam says: 2:46:43 PM

lol!

Shauna Nicholson says: 2:47:08 PM

Where I'm going to lunch; great articles or resources; photos of events I'm attending; conversations with others about, well, everything!

David R Haslam says: 2:47:39 PM

 and yes you do!!

   2:47:52 PM

Q8. Any advice that you would like to share?

Shauna Nicholson says: 2:48:55 PM

Listen and learn from your network; choose who you follow with care; don't spam or try to sell; make sure to meet OFFLINE, too!

David R Haslam says: 2:49:51 PM

Q9. Your best Twitter experience?

Shauna Nicholson says: 2:50:11 PM

Getting my job!

David R Haslam says: 2:50:23 PM

lol

Shauna Nicholson says: 2:50:32 PM

want the story?

David R Haslam says: 2:50:45 PM

yes please ☺

Shauna Nicholson says: 2:52:15 PM

Out of college, I took the first salary and benfits job I could find. The economy was less than desirable ('07) and that made me nervous.

2:53:01 PM

After going to school for technical communication, I never thought of myself as a marketer, though I had ended up doing a lot of freelance in that area.

2:53:28 PM

Long story short, I took a job I now refer to as my "Office Space" job, sat in my cubicle and accepted my adult fate.

2:54:46 PM

Though unapproved, I started marketing through social media. First with forums and then it grew. After a while, I started building a network of people as passionate as I was becoming about online marketing (while, at the time, I was primarily consumed with offline).

2:55:31 PM

A friend, who was also unhappy with her job, put in her notice and set off to find one that would make her happy--WITHOUT FINDING A NEW JOB FIRST!

2:56:40 PM

I was stunned and inspired. That week, I attended my first Tweetup and met some incredible people, including @chrisbrogan @kenbubary @jwphillips, and others. A week later, after an inspiring chat with new friends, I had put in my notice.

2:57:06 PM

Thursday of week 1, I had lunch with @charliecurve, @tomcurve and @terrybean.

2:57:34 PM

Knowning my passions and skillset, hey recommended me to @kevinbiznet (who was just Kevin Krason back then).

David R Haslam says: 2:58:46 PM

wow... i'm on the edge of my seat! 😊 continue...

Shauna Nicholson says: 2:59:03 PM

Without my knowledge, Twitter friends had called Kevin and Dave to recommend me. I interviewed with @kevinbiznet and @davebiznet on Thursday of week 2. They called me on my drive home and offered me the position.

2:59:15 PM

I started the following Monday, never missing a day of work.

3:00:08 PM

(end)

David R Haslam says: 3:00:54 PM

I'm not sure we are still connected

3:02:59 PM

wow!

3:03:04 PM

very cool...

Shauna Nicholson says: 3:03:08 PM

haha

3:03:11 PM

i think i'm done

David R Haslam says: 3:03:28 PM

lol... can't be sure with you! 😊

3:03:34 PM

ok

Shauna Nicholson says: 3:03:55 PM

Basically, I built the network before I knew I'd need it

3:04:22 PM

And now, I'm very happy!

David R Haslam says: 3:04:52 PM

I know, and your enthusiasm is catching!!

Shauna Nicholson says: 3:04:55 PM

Thanks 😊

David R Haslam says: 3:05:05 PM

yw!

3:05:09 PM

Q10. Top three Tweeps that you would recommend?

Shauna Nicholson says: 3:05:16 PM

Hm

3:05:25 PM

That really depends on what you're looking for.

3:05:37 PM

I don't want to offend people, hah

David R Haslam says: 3:05:42 PM

what ever you think...

Shauna Nicholson says: 3:05:48 PM

Okay...

David R Haslam says: 3:05:52 PM
and that is OK as an answer

Shauna Nicholson says: 3:05:59 PM
Okay thanks

David R Haslam says: 3:06:11 PM

lol.... off the hook! 😄

    3:06:16 PM

ok...

    3:06:57 PM

Q11. Other social networks you use regularly?

Shauna Nicholson says: 3:07:06 PM
Facebook

    3:07:22 PM

Tumblr

    3:07:28 PM

Pandora

    3:07:35 PM

LinkedIn

    3:07:46 PM

BusinessWeek

    3:07:57 PM

Yelp

    3:08:05 PM

MySpace, kind of

    3:08:11 PM

YouTube

3:08:16 PM

Vimeo
Flickr

3:08:33 PM

I think I may have a problem, hahah.

David R Haslam says: 3:08:52 PM

And that's why you are the Princess of SM 😊

3:08:58 PM

lol, that too!!

Shauna Nicholson says: 3:09:02 PM

Oh, thank you!

David R Haslam says: 3:09:55 PM

Princess in a positive way too. If I called you the Queen, people would age you too much!

3:10:17 PM

Q12. What do you think your future is with Twitter?

Shauna Nicholson says: 3:11:01 PM

I'll continue to develop a QUALITY (not quantity-heavy) network. I downloaded Power Twitter, so now I don't even have to click links.

3:11:19 PM

I use it to gather advice for purchases and business issues.

David R Haslam says: 3:12:00 PM

could you expand on that a little?

Shauna Nicholson says: 3:12:41 PM

I'm constantly learning for others; the way they do things; products they recommend...

3:13:00 PM

My fellow users are genuine people, and great friends.

3:14:18 PM

I always seem to meet them offline, eventually, and it's great to see someone new (for example @ambercadabra) who immediately hugs me and says "we're best friends already!"

3:15:00 PM

As opposed to, say, faceless brands, whose life is not all that relevant, informational, or familiar to me.

3:15:08 PM

There's no relationship there.

David R Haslam says: 3:15:30 PM

very good! ☺

3:15:51 PM

any final thoughts for the "formal" interview?

Shauna Nicholson says: 3:16:29 PM

Know and love your third party Twitter apps!

3:16:32 PM

Thanks, David!

David R Haslam says: 3:16:44 PM

lol...

3:16:52 PM

yw Shauna!

Shauna Nicholson says: 3:16:55 PM

Okay off to a meeting. Have a great day!

David R Haslam says: 3:17:16 PM

and you! I'll e-mail you later! ☺ and thank you!

Shauna Nicholson says: 3:17:31 PM

Great ☺

Part 2 – Why use Twitter?

"He who has a why can endure any how."
    - Friedrich Nietzsche

Chapter 3 – To Twitter, or Not To Twitter

"All the world's a stage,
And all men and women merely players…"
- *William Shakespeare (As You Like It, Jacques, Act II, Scene VII)*

…that is NOT the question! Deciding if you want to become a Tweep or not shouldn't be a big decision in your life. The real question is how much time you want to put into it, and what are you prepared to offer to people who may follow you.

Twitter is similar to all the social network tools on the internet in that it is *social*; the central theme of this book and Twitter in general. It is difficult to discuss decisions about Twitter without discussing the whole social networking topic in general. Twitter is a very narrowly focused tool in terms of what it can do, but very powerful in how it can be used. Think of Twitter as a knife, and almost every other type of social media tool as being forks, spoons, and chopsticks. All cultures can claim that their forks, spoons, and chopsticks are all you need to eat a meal. But, if you took their knives away, then those cultures would be out of action very quickly, as they would not be able to prepare the meal. Twitter is another knife. It gets down to THE fundamental of lasting communication: The written word.

Cave paintings, clay tablets, papyrus, paper, the printing press, telegraph, telephone, faxing, e-mailing, text messaging, ***and now Twitter***, transmit the message to others. That is all these systems do. And how essential is that? Permanent communication is THE difference between us and every other species on the planet. Twitter accomplishes it simply and with the minimum amount of fuss.

There are three areas to consider when using Twitter:

1. Personal use
2. Professional use
3. Cautions when using

There are many strategies to consider. Choosing the right one for you may not be clear at once. That's OK. When you read the case studies, you'll find that most of the people interviewed did not know the purpose Twitter would serve for them when they began exploring it. Some even stopped using it for a while.

Before you read the more detailed explanations ahead, and since this IS a work book, here is some work for you. ☺

What would you consider using Twitter for?

1. Alternative / supplement to texting?   Y / N
2. Keeping friends / family informed?   Y / N
3. Holding conversations that are permanent?   Y / N
4. Giving and getting travel reports?   Y / N
5. Checking the financial markets?   Y / N
6. Weather reports?   Y / N
7. News updates?   Y / N
8. Sports updates?   Y / N
9. School closing information?   Y / N
10. Airport arrival and departure information?   Y / N
11. Concert ticket availability?   Y / N
12. Local event calendars?   Y / N
13. Checking on your cats?   Y / N
14. Internet shopping?   Y / N
15. Discount programs for IRL stores?   Y / N
16. Hotel availability?   Y / N
17. Recipes?   Y / N
18. Inspirational quotations?   Y / N
19. Knitting patterns?   Y / N
20. Design / creative ideas?   Y / N
21. Brain storming with the planet?   Y / N
22. Asking questions?   Y / N
23. Giving answers?   Y / N
24. Lifting your mood and getting inspired?   Y / N
25. Inspiring others?   Y / N
26. Finding the best coffee / meal in town?   Y / N
27. Find a job?   Y / N
28. Find a house?   Y / N
29. Find a car?   Y / N
30. Have fun?   Y / N
31. _____   Y / N

Case Study 3 – The Connectors

"Creativity is the power to connect the seemingly unconnected."
  - *William Plomer*

Ever have one of those "a-ha" moments? No, I'm not talking about hearing "Take On Me" coming on the radio... <u>LOL</u>! Now I'm showing my age! What I mean is that moment, which happens seemingly by chance, when your life changes forever! One such moment happened to my good friend Nancy Zychowicz (known as Nancy Z throughout Toastmasters, and "our Nancy" to a very small group indeed!) On April 1st, 2008, Nancy was attending a speech competition in Ann Arbor, Michigan. The "a-ha" moment occurred when she was introduced to two people that were visiting their first Toastmasters event. After an incredible but brief conversation, Nancy resumed her duties at the competition. About an hour later, Nancy made a brief, life changing phone call, as she drove home to Toledo, <u>Ohio</u>.

Since that night was a Tuesday, as was almost always the case, I had spent a great evening at Dearborn Dynamic Toastmasters in Livonia, Michigan, about 30 miles from where Nancy had been. Towards the end of the meeting, my cell phone rang. It is good form in Toastmasters meetings, as it should be in ALL meetings, that my phone was in vibrate mode, so it did not disturb anyone. And, also in good form, I did not check my phone until an opportune time. I left the meeting, sat in my car, and then checked the message.

I saw the call was from Nancy. I then heard an excited tale about two amazing people she'd met in Ann Arbor that evening. She gave me their names and a number to call.

The following afternoon, I was in Ann Arbor myself to give a speech entitled "Why Are You Here?" Its subject was *why we volunteer to give our time*, and *how it is better to support and encourage people rather than stand in their way.* It is just amazing how things come together. As I drove back home in the mid-afternoon, I remembered Nancy's message from the night before. On arrival at home I called the number. It rang, and rang, and rang. Nothing. That was that.

The morning of Thursday, April 3rd 2008 was uneventful, other than one thing. I dialed that number again. This time, the call was answered: "InSights Group, how can I help you?" a friendly young woman's voice was on the line.

"Hi! Can I speak to Sandy Maki or Al Curtis please?" I inquired. "Sandy speaking!" began yet another amazing, life-changing series of event for me. Just later that day, I visited the InSights Group and my life has been filled with social networking (both virtual AND real life) ever since!

The concept behind the InSights Group is hard to define because it is allowed to evolve. Basically they provide a networking and business services hub for people within driving distance of Brighton, Michigan (and beyond). InSights Group was founded in January 2008. At their first event, they had five people. At their first anniversary meeting, they had 105! And the number of members continues to grow! Sandy and Al truly typify what has become the norm within online social networking. Creativity, positivity, sharing, and caring! They are natural magnets for people and connected to so many networking circles and groups.

Most of the InSights Group events are at their facilities. But Sandy and Al will break the bonds occasionally and venture forth to other events. Here is what they have to say about Twitter. First, Sandy:

1).   Twitter ID:
       @SandiMaki

2).   Personal or corporate use:
       "Interesting question! At first glance I would say corporate. But as we teach people in our social media classes, it is important to market yourself, meaning that you should focus on the personal side. When I use Twitter, all roads lead to my online house, which is my blog and website. And that means it combines the personal and corporate side of me. So, the true answer to the question is both."

3).   Did you try anything similar before Twitter?
       "I had been using Facebook, LinkedIn, and group sites before I got involved in Twitter. I didn't start blogging until after Twitter. Twitter and full blown blogging kind of started together. Now when I update my blog it automatically posts update messages on Twitter and Facebook. It eases the social networking load by doing this."

4). Who introduced you to it?

"Wow! Let me think! Not sure I remember exactly. My early Twitter experience was with people like you (David) and Charlie Wollborg Tweeting DURING meetings. I was interested why you where doing it and that is what got me started."

5). When did you start?

"Probably in Oct / Nov of 2008"

6). Why do you use Twitter?

"It does several things for me. It let's me take a peek at what's being said and what is going on in the world. It provides nice shiny stuff. Twitter let's me see cool things that people are doing and sharing. The trending topics are great to find new things quickly. It's also a world wide news source. I teach about social media, so I like to see how people are using it for that "getting to know you" soft marketing approach. I like that Twitter enables me to promote my blog, and also helps to publicize people that are following me. A favorite element is seeing what people are re-Tweeting of mine, or the ability to follow conversations that I've been involved in."

7). What do you Tweet about?

"I Tweet about things I find interesting: web sites, YouTube videos that are cool, neat events and local happenings that I will be part of. While I'm teaching social media, I usually Tweet about the particular topic I'm teaching in the class. I always avoid the shameless plugs etc. Marketing and selling on Twitter is all about relationships, not the hard sell. I also like to respond to questions that people ask if I have an answer for them."

8). Any advice that you would like to share?

"When using Twitter to market, make sure the Tweet includes all the info someone needs. If you are having a conversation, make sure you include a hash-tag or URL for additional information that they might need. If you use Twitter and Facebook, you should help to initiate conversations of the activities of your friends. For example, if you know Tom is working on a new web site, ask him how it is coming along. Engage him in a conversation. Create business community growth through growth of the individual members. Another key aspect is your Twitter profile. A fun and quirky profile is great, but if you are using it for business, use your bio to help explain more about you and your company, and what may be found on your website. Also, use Twitter frequently. If you don't log in every day, use blog feeds to populate Twitter. The main thing is to have a presence. We advise a student of the class that with so many social network avenues, being active on all of them becomes impossible. However, having a presence is essential if you are marketing on the internet. With Twitter, regular updates are far more important than more static sites such as LinkedIn."

9). Your best Twitter experience?

"The best experience I've had so far was when Colin Thomas from MLIVE.com sent me a link a couple of months ago. The link showed a woman in the audience at a Gary Vaynerchuck presentation. She was talking about how to promote the '100,000 Hugs' campaign that was going around the world. Shortly after, I picked up a copy of 'Tribes' by Seth Godin on the recommendation of another friend. I read the book straight through! In the book, Godin also mentioned Gary V. Then I somehow got to follow the '100,000 Hugs' campaign on Twitter, and before too long I had a direct message from Gail Lynne Goodwin. She is the woman in Gary V's audience talking about the hugs! It is a small world that is getting smaller!"

10).   Top three Tweeps that you would recommend?
"At first, I'd follow anyone of interest to me. But once I hit the Twitter follower limit, I changed to a mainly Michigan follower strategy. Now, I follow people that are important to the business climate here in Michigan, members of the InSights Group, and then interesting people on the national stage. Because our business model is about connecting people in the local area, the local area is where we focus. As to narrowing it to just three people I follow, that may be another story!"

11).   Other social networks you use regularly?
"I use Facebook mostly, but I'm also active on LinkedIn, InSights Group site, and YouTube. It is best to create profiles on ALL social networks that you can, but concentrate being active on a few. I use Ping.fm to automate feeds from my blog, which helps generate interest on other sites."

12).   What do you think your future with Twitter will be?
"Teaching people to use it is my main current activity with Twitter. My next plan will be helping to promote more education for local businesses using the InSights Organic Marketing Program. Beyond that is following in your footsteps David, and producing a book on the InSights Organic Marketing Program."

And now, Al:

1).   Twitter ID:
@allancurtis

2).   Personal or corporate use:
"Corporate use"

3).   Did you try anything similar before Twitter?
"No"

4).   Who introduced you to it?
"I'm not entirely sure. Pre-Twitter is a blur."

5).   When did you start?
"September / October 2008"

6).   Why do you use Twitter?
"Because it's cool. The philosophy of Twitter is to create a real person on the other end of the communication. It is a very real and genuine form of social networking. Other social networking tools tend to be past and present based, where as Twitter concentrates on the now and the future. I like that. People live IN the now."

7).   What do you Tweet about?
"Most of my Tweets are about events that are happening now or in the future along with personal thoughts for the day."

8).   Any advice that you would like to share?
"First and foremost be authentic and be your real self. Twitter is not about direct promotion. Tease people into wanting to know more about you. Create energy around you so that people want to get to know you. It is not the quantity but the quality of your followers that matters and are they the right demographic for your business. Pre-thinking what you want to do, and how to use it to support your business is important. If you have a local business, follow local people. If you have an international business, follow people in your target market. Also, prolific Tweeters may not always be good, and this may not be an effective marketing strategy. A Tweep with a balance between Followers, Following, and Updates

tends to be someone who understands the power of Twitter to influence people. Be selective in who you follow."

9).   Your best Twitter experience?

"Some one from Missouri who had the exact same name (including the unusual spelling of Allan) contacted me on Twitter. We are both descended from Curtis' in Ohio, and he led me to an interesting web site about the Curtis family name. You never know what possibilities may arise."

10).   Top three Tweeps that you would recommend?

"@GaryV for sure. He has a good grasp on social media.

@sandimaki First Lady of the InSights Group!

@skydiver the HARO guy

@terrybean and @charliecurve from Motor City Connect"

11).   Other social networks you use regularly?

"My main ones are LinkedIn, Facebook. Also, I use InSights-Group, Ping.FM, Ning, and seven or eight CollectiveX platforms."

12).   What do you think your future with Twitter will be?

"As I learn to develop strategic formats, I will become even more effective. Grouping of people is essential: target markets, local communities, target demographics, tribes."

Chapter 4 – Personal Twitter

"Pessimism is an excuse for not trying and a guarantee to a personal failure"
 - Bill Clinton

1. The Texting Habit

My daughter Deanna is turning, well, a certain age this year… She will be 30, but please don't tell her I said that! However, back in the mid-90s, she was an extremely social high school student. In those days (LOL! 15 years ago sounds like 150 years ago from a communication technology stand point!), she had a 'beeper' (if you don't know what a beeper or pager is, ask your parents). I, as any good parent would, told her that if she wanted to have this new necessity of modern life, she had to pay for it herself. So that is what she did. My baby girl went out and got a job to pay for her beeper habit!

Her first beeper received numbers only. Very quickly after she bought the first one, the number of beeps she got in an afternoon skyrocketed! Social networking in action, '90's style! Of course, she would then have to get on the phone to call the person back. Fortunately, we had free local calling so cost was not an issue there. However, the competition for phone time was fierce! Our oldest son had friends to talk to, *and so did we*. We restricted the children to one hour a day on the phone during the week, and two hours on weekends and vacations. In short order, my daughter signed up for more hours at work to pay for her own phone line. She now had unlimited use of her phone line. Soon the battle lines shifted again. Increased phone time led to a decrease in homework effort, which in turn resulted in declining grades. The policy became two hours a day on her phone although it is amazing how much extra phone time can be achieved if you learn to whisper, or call when your parents are asleep!

My daughter also used her beeper as a fashion accessory. If she could not upgrade its functionality, she could always upgrade its appearance. Changing her beeper was just like changing any other part of her wardrobe (while my daughter has never been a big one for jewelry, she certainly does pay attention to clothing). However, technology moved along. The low cost, small sized, convenient cell (or mobile if you are non-North American) phone replaced the beeper for most people in the early 2000's. (It amuses me to see beepers still in use in medical based TV shows). My daughter routinely updates her cell phone for both features and looks. The cell phone took over the mantle of the beeper with the ubiquitous text message. And that strikes me as interesting too. Deanna still sends and receives texts. A text is still a better idea in a lot of circumstances than a brief phone conversation. It is still a permanent form of communication. A phone conversation is not (unless of course you are being subject to a wire-tap, or "this call maybe recorded for quality assurance purposes").

Text messaging is typically a very personal thing. In fact, it is usually "person-to-person". Some of the most effective use of Twitter is also the "person-to-person" conversation. The big difference is that all your followers can read your side of the conversation, and the followers of the other person can read theirs. *Or so it may seem...* To have a private conversation, you can Direct Message (DM) the person you are talking to. Then you can talk as long as you want. (My graphics artist, @EleArt, and I had a DM conversation lasting several days as we worked on the cover of the book. We found it THE most efficient way to quickly, concisely, and permanently record the work we are doing together).

Twitter has the advantage of traditional cell phone texting, combined with being stored on the internet, and not just on the user's phone. Yes! You can receive and send Tweets on your mobile devices.

2. The Proud Grandparents

Grandparents can be wonderful! They have a unique way to love and care for you. While parents should always put your welfare first, grandparents can 'let it slide' sometimes... Now that we have five grand children with number six arriving at about the same time as this book, I better understand the behavior of my grandparents. [Update: Cali Helena was born on May 20th, 2009. Number six HAS arrived! ☺]

Grandparents perform three major tasks (outside of unconditional love for their grand children!):

1. Perspective on the past
2. Hope for the future
3. Communication center for the entire family

You can use Twitter in each of these three ways. It is common to see discussions on Twitter about current events. This leads into analysis and perspective based on the past. The advantage with reading such Tweets is that you can get a wide range of views which most other sources do not provide. With social networking in all forms, it is always best to keep an open mind. If you do, you never know what you might find!

A powerful and positive effect of Twitter is its influence on your future! Meeting new people is part of how your personal future is built. Always have a day full of WOW (wonderful opportunities waiting, words of wisdom, World of Warcraft, Wings of War, or Wide Open West depending on your point of view!) Tweeps will Tweet about the latest trends in all sorts of areas. They will give you advice or help guide when you ask. Charlie Wolborg of Curve Detroit said it best about the big three social networks: "Facebook is your past, LinkedIn is your now, and Twitter is your future!"

If you wanted good news to spread when you were a child, you'd call Grandma. She'd do the rest! Now, you have Twitter! Tell the Twitterverse about your good news! As long as you are not direct selling, any positive news you have about yourself can be spread far, wide, and fast! So go for it! Spread the joy!

3. Say What You Are Doing!

The power of suggestion is amazing! When you read something your subconscious takes hold of it. It can bend and shape your future thoughts and actions. And with only 140 characters in a Tweet, the mind has a bite size morsel to play with!

Let's try a little experiment. Read the following sentence three times. Pause for a few moments. Turn to the next page and continue reading:

"I just had a wonderful cup of coffee in my favorite place!"

"I just had a wonderful cup of coffee in my favorite place!"

"I just had a wonderful cup of coffee in my favorite place!"

Are you thinking about a wonderful cup of coffee for yourself right now? Which style did you think of, and where would you get it? How much are you willing to pay for it? Or if you prefer another beverage, are you thinking about that? And how about the 'place'? A coffee shop? Your kitchen, office, or maybe Grandma's house? Were your thoughts pleasant?

Think about what you do in your personal life (but not necessarily private life). Tweet about it! The power of your suggestion may just trigger reactions in other people. How about the clubs, groups, and associations that you belong to? Tweeting about them will encourage others to join in. For example, Tweet about sports teams you like. I have been influenced by this. I'm a life long Manchester United Football Club fan. When Tony Meehan, also known as @mancityalerts, began following me, I returned the favor. Now, dare I say it, I have become interested in Manchester City FC. Yikes! ☺ Red Devils, you are still my number one!

If you let the Twitterverse know what you are doing, what things are important to you, and what your passions are, people will be interested!

Case Study 4 – Aging Backwards

"Aging is not 'lost youth' but a new stage of opportunity and strength."
- *Betty Friedan*

Jackie Silver is one of the most enthusiastic and dynamic practitioners of the use of Twitter that I've met. I say 'met'… and yet Jackie and I know each other only through Twitter and phone calls so far. We have not been face-to-face or IRL ('in real life' as Jackie likes to say) *yet*!

I can pinpoint to the hour when Jackie and I first spoke. On the morning of February 16th, 2009, Jackie sent out a Tweet. She said that she did not understand how the TweetDeck application (see Chapter 5, Part 2 for details on TweetDeck) worked with groups of Tweeps. I offered to help by setting a phone call for the following morning. At 11:00 am, we talked for the first time! And what a dazzling conversation it was!

As you will see below, Jackie truly lives by the philosophy of helping others whenever she can. We talked for 45 minutes. After a ten minute discussion about TweetDeck, the conversation switched to life, the universe, and everything. She pointed the way to write the book that you are currently reading! She told me all about how she got her book ("Aging Backwards: Secrets to Staying Young" of course! ☺) published, how she goes about making presentations, radio, and TV appearances, and her voice-over work. We talked of families, friends, and of course Twitter. Jackie was excited to be interviewed for this book. So here it is!

1). Twitter ID:
@AgingBackwards

2). Personal or corporate use:
"My personal and corporate lives are intertwined. This is because 'Aging Backwards' IS my personal brand. I live my brand. Socializing and connecting on Twitter helps create awareness for my brand, but first and foremost Twitter is about personal connections. That's what I love about it."

3). Did you try anything similar before Twitter?
"I did not try any social media before this. And I'm not really 'trying' when I use it, but I simply enjoy using Twitter. I'm not what they call a social media maven... I have a Facebook account but rarely use it. Twitter is where I live in the social media world."

4). Who introduced you to it?
"I don't remember ☺. I'm on the web 24/7. I probably came across it during research on one of my projects. I may have read about it in a blog or a web news report. I'm just not sure exactly."

5). When did you start?
"I think it was around May / June 2008. The first time I looked at Twitter I didn't get it. I thought it was perhaps a big waste of time, or maybe even nonsensical. But, something drew me back. I gave it a second chance. And I was pleased to discover I was SO WRONG! I'm

extremely grateful that I did give Twitter that second look because then I became a 'Twaddict,' LOL."

6).   Why do you use Twitter?
"One of my early Tweets explains it best: 'Twitter is like every party I ever and never went to!' You see, a good party is always full of fun people with interesting conversations. You can step into and out of the action any time you want. Just like all the best parties, if you need to go for a drink or leave a good conversation for some other reason, you can re-join the party later, and know there will be someone great to talk to. Twitter is just like that. I also use Twitter because it's fun! I've come across so many amazing, interesting, and upbeat people. I also learn a lot. Twitter gives me instant access to all kinds of information and experts on a wide variety of subjects. Honestly, I don't think there is any one place on the web that gathers together so many experts with so much generosity. People on Twitter tend to give more than they receive, and I love that. In addition, it is so simple! Twitter is clean and easy, and fits into my hectic life! It also follows the mantra that collaboration is the new competition! I've always been someone who enjoys the spirit of cooperation."

7).   What do you Tweet about?
"LOL! I Tweet about everything! My life, my son, my workouts, Aging Backwards, and just engaging in conversations with my Twitter friends. I don't Tweet about politics. I don't care to talk about in real life either, so I avoid it on Twitter too."

8).   Any advice that you would like to share?
"Tone it down on the SELL, SELL, SELL! It's all about relationships on Twitter. There is a time and a place for selling, and Twitter is not it. I don't care for auto-

responders either. I don't want to be corresponding with a robot...unless he's really cute! LOL."

9).   Your best Twitter experience?

"I've had so many great experiences. The best experience is the continuous one. Generosity and authenticity. That's what it is all about!"

10).   Top three Tweeps that you would recommend?

"I love ALL my Tweeps! I recommend ALL OF THEM!"

11).   Other social networks you use regularly?

"Twitter is the only one that has ever appealed to me. I use Skype as a great communication tool. I use it to transfer large files instantaneously to people. Skype is pretty amazing too, but it's not really a 'social network'."

12).   What do you think your future with Twitter will be?

"I guess that depends on the future of Twitter itself. If it stays generous, sharing, and positive, I believe my friendships and connections will grow. And there will be even more new and exciting opportunities to come."

Chapter 5 – Professional Twitter

"Professionalism is knowing how to do it, when to do it, and doing it."
 - *Frank Tyger*

1. Intelligent Tweeting

Although Twitter recommends that *you tell what you are doing*, one of the best ways to make use of Twitter is to be inquisitive. Ask plenty of questions and give plenty of answers. By asking questions, you can engage people in interesting conversations in addition to finding the answers you need. The questions themselves will attract followers that can either provide the answer, or are interested in a similar question. Asking a question shows that you are active and interested. And that is important.

Answering questions is even more important. This shows that you have knowledge, and are the potential "go-to person" in that field. But never ever lie or knowingly give an answer that you are not 100% sure of. If you consistently give out false information you will loose all credibility. That is even worse than being a wallflower and saying nothing. Also, avoid being a bore. If all you ever do is answering others' questions without any other Tweets, you may find your follower stream drying up.

Balancing between asking and answering is important. But like everything else in the Twitterverse, don't worry about it too much. You can always change your ways to find the style that best suits you...

2. Making Proposals

Along similar lines to asking questions, is using Twitter to request specific business help. If you are preparing to spend money for yourself or your organization, and you do not have a current supplier, you can use Twitter to help.

Take a look at the cover of this book. It is an example of this. I had put a request for quote (RFQ) out on Twitter in the early part of 2009. As a result Elena got in contact with me. I looked at her website, and was very happy with her work. We stayed in touch and when I was looking for a cover designer she said she was interested.

The other side of this equation is that people are always looking for help with their business on Twitter. The key here is that you must stay engaged and read other Tweets to make sure you see the opportunities. They are there. Searching can help dig out the requests of others too. Be creative, and you'll find what you are looking for.

3. How to Brand

Twitter is such a universal tool; it is sometimes difficult to narrow things down to "professional" use. The organization you represent could be a company, non-profit, civic group, library, space program, or just yourself. Branding applies no matter what. You can blend Twitter into your existing branding strategy. For your branding efforts to be most effective, you need to combine Twitter with other areas.

For example, while attending trade shows, conferences, or workshops related to your organization, make sure you send Tweets out about the event. People will know where you are and what you are doing, and see how involved you are in the community. As a result, it will raise your brand profile. In addition, the event organizers will tend to be VERY happy.

Sharing information concerning your organization and things that affect it is also good. Re-Tweeting interesting posts from other Tweeps, or Tweeting web links of concern to your organization is fine. Doing this shows that you are supportive, active, and informed to the news of your business.

Building your brand and increasing its recognition also involves communication with others. Whenever possible engage other Tweeps in conversations. Be interested in them particularly if they are in a field related to your organization. As you communicate others will notice, and your presence will extend.

4. The Soft Sell

A common theme in social networking is avoiding the 'hard sell'. It is not all about me. It is all about we. People decide if they want to follow you on Twitter. If you are too pushy with yourself or your product / service, people will stop following you, and your message will get nowhere.

Being informative and interesting are far more important. Encouraging and supporting others will endear you to the people you are connected with. This will lead to you being the person others think of when they need problems solved. And that will lead to sales.

There are some other interesting business models on Twitter. On Twitter, search for @woot. This is a classic example of bucking the trend. Instead of avoiding the 'hard sell', @woot embraces it! On their web site (www.woot.com) they have one featured product. The @woot sends out a Tweet about that product. It stays on the web site until it is sold out. Does this work as a strategy? Well, @woot currently has over 600,000 followers, and therefore over 600,000 will get the message that they are selling X product for Y price.

Other retail locations make similar use of Twitter to run temporary specials or to inform of particular events. But in general, caution should be applied to this method. Few like physical junk mail or e-mail spam. (Exceptions are printers, the post office, data storage companies, direct marketers, and the lumber industry). If you use Twitter to just advertise in a new way, you might be wasting your time. But, if this method works for you, Woot!

5. Be the CEO

CEO's should be the leaders of their organizations. Twitter gives ANYONE an opportunity to lead. That does not mean usurping the role of the CEO. It can mean that leadership talent can surface more easily if the organization adopts Twitter as a corporate communication tool.

CEO's should be aware of all their organizations strategic activities. But more than that, they need to be the leader rather than just the manager. Twitter allows you to lead the thoughts of the people who follow you. This can be powerful. Make sure that those thoughts are positive and support your professional message.

If you are in a leadership position / role, Twitter can be used to communicate with all levels of your organization. Because of its ability to cut through layers of management, Twitter can enable a CEO to lead the whole organization more effectively.

It is also worth checking what others are saying about you. A member of staff who is upset can do a lot of damage to the image you are trying to promote. With social networks, such disgruntled staff can spread the negative message wide and fast. Always monitor your companies image on the social networks, and counter-act 'bad press' as fast as you can.

Case Study 5 – A Good Cup of Joe with the CEO!

"A cup of coffee commits one to forty years of friendship."
        - Turkish Proverb

Being English, I love a good cup of tea. But living in the USA, I'm surrounded by coffee. Coffee drinkers, coffee products, coffee shops! Even my Tweeps talk about the benefits of that first morning sip from a good cup of Joe.

The coffee shop / house was been a universal place of commerce and friendship for over 500 years! Ever since the first one was opened in Istanbul (then Constantinople), Turkey in 1457 the world has been a different place.

In southeast Michigan we have a wide variety of coffee shops to choose from. One particular chain has become a favorite with the local social network crowd. When you step into a Biggby Coffee, you are in for a different experience. Bright, cheerful, and friendly are hallmarks of Biggby and fortunately for me, they serve more than just coffee.

In mid-January 2009, I arranged two business meetings at a Biggby in Novi, Michigan. That January morning my first experience walking into the store was as if I was a long lost friend coming to visit. A call of "Hello, how are you?" came from behind the counter. As I approached the staff engaged me in a conversation. I felt very welcome. I ordered my caramel hot chocolate and turkey bagel and settled down to wait for my visitors.

After the meetings had finished, I sent out a Tweet about my experience with the store. I packed up my laptop and headed home. **Within ten minutes**, @BiggbyBob replied to me on Twitter, thanking me for visiting the store! *That is listening to AND engaging customers!*

Bob Fish (aka @BiggbyBob) and I began following each other on that day. Bob is a thoroughly modern CEO, with a very creative approach to his business. Born in Germany, he lived in Europe for twelve years. He manages to make a blend of different cultures in his business life. He is a graduate of Michigan State University and opened the first Biggby Coffee in March 1995 near the university in East Lansing.

The growth of Biggby has been spectacular! Every two years, the number of stores has approximately doubled. 1997 saw the second Biggby. In 1998 they setup franchise operations. That changed everything! In 2000, they had seven stores under the banner. By 2004, the number was at 26, and by 2008, Biggby opened its 105th store.

Bob best described his use of social networking as giving 'personality' to the corporation and Twitter exemplifies this. Biggby Coffee aims to take customer satisfaction to a higher level, where the mode of operation turns to customer INTERACTION!

The way Bob uses Twitter allows him to do something that is almost unique: the CEO of the company interacting directly with the customers. By doing this, and other activities such as 'Spot BiggyBob', he connects to the customers as much as possible. It is not only building traditional customer loyalty, but also concern and interest in the success of Biggby Coffee.

Twitter allows communication channels to be consolidated. Traditionally, different audiences may have been handled by different groups. Sales, marketing, technical, production, and HR could be giving conflicting meanings to customers, prospects, internal departments, finance, and the company staff at large. If Twitter is used at a high level of the company, one clear message can be given to all concerned.

When I asked Bob for an interview for this book, he invited me over to his 'office'. It took place in the most unusual coffee shop I had ever been in. Biggby Coffee corporate headquarters are on the third floor of a very average looking office building in East Lansing, Michigan. However, the offices themselves are anything but ordinary.

Having arrived in a fairly standard reception area, I was then escorted to the Biggby Training Center. Entering the room, I found it was a perfect Biggby Coffee shop, apart from three details: a. No customers, b. No staff, and c. @BiggbyBob sat at a table using his laptop. After Bob personally prepared a caramel hot chocolate for me we settled down for the interview.

1).   Twitter ID:
       @BiggbyBob

2).   Personal or corporate use:
       "I use it for both."

3). Did you try anything similar before Twitter?

"The first thing I tried that was similar was www.biggbybob.com in March 2008. This is a blog of some of my activities. It chronicles my visits to the stores. I also interview employees and customers, and use video updates when I can. I use it to articulate in a fun way who and what Biggby is. But I found it burdensome for constant use. I still update it, but not as frequently. My next social network was Facebook. Again, I maintain a presence there, but it is not my main avenue. We also developed www.bhappylounge.com as a fun place to allow customers and staff to interact."

4). Who introduced you to it?

"I'm not exactly sure. A local company called Artemis helped to create the BHappyLounge. A web developer from there told me about Twitter. I was not sure what to do with it at first. I just stumbled through. There were no manuals or support systems back then."

5). When did you start?

"April 2008"

6). Why do you use Twitter?

"I use Twitter to help promote brand values rather than the brand itself. Biggby Coffee cultural values are:

Be happy
Have fun
Make friends
Love people
Drink great coffee

Twitter helps to achieve all these.

However, Twitter is not the whole story. We also have 'one take' videos on YouTube and the blog. It is WHAT THE BRAND IS. It is not what is the brand? If Biggby was a car, what would it be? My answer is an inclusive one. Not exclusive. Biggby is high quality, but it is more Minivan than Mercedes. Families prefer minivans."

7). What do you Tweet about?

"For personal use, I Tweet about running, going out with M (Michele, my wife), seeing a movie, asking for travel advice. I always Tweet about where I am. Professionally, I'll Tweet about promoting events, and interacting with the staff and customers."

8). Any advice that you would like to share?

"No ranting and raving on Twitter. Keep it real and the real HAS TO BE real. Don't forget, Twitter is accessible by everyone! This includes employees, customers, suppliers, operators, etc. So any message on any social media has to be the truth!! Most marketers think of it as a communication challenge to customers, but it is more than that. By using my @BiggbyBob persona, I can share my message DIRECTLY with franchise employees, rather than the traditional of mail and e-mail, through the franchise organizations.

Being true and honest at all levels of the organization is essential in social media.

One other important aspect we teach when showing our organization how to use social media is 'Don't forget to fly the plane.' All too often in a crisis, people tend to under or over respond. But whatever you do, you always have to fly the plane.

Biggby Coffee is retail. In any retail operation you should treat the customer like a friend walking into your house. Always greet them, and offer them a drink, a bite to eat. Twitter can be used to extend that concept when they leave the store.

People intend to do social media right, but don't know where to go with it. Start with who YOU are. Be interesting, engaging, and personal. If you are not prepared to do these things, use a web site for your marketing and information. Before you start with it, you have to know WHO YOU ARE!

At Biggby Coffee, we have done this by defining our core values. These are:

Energy, excitement, enthusiasm
Faith, confidence, courage
Return on involvement (the new ROI)
PE ratio – positive energy
Newton's 3rd law (every action has an equal and opposite reaction)

I use a conscious decision not to force followers… I'll follow anyone who mentions Biggby and is interesting in an organic way. I will not follow a mass of people. Twitter is founded on interaction, not blind spam. Without the interaction, there is no value and there is no point!"

9).   Your best Twitter experience?
"Choosing a best is really hard. With 3,000+ friends on Twitter, it is difficult to say. I think in general, the best experiences are when people trust me enough to tell me their bad experiences. This leads to ways to improve our products and our interaction with the customers."

10). Top three Tweeps that you would recommend?
@DaveBenjamin
@damnredhead
@susanorchard
@davesacre
"I know that's four, but I just can't choose just three!"

11). Other social networks you use regularly?
"www.BiggbyBob.com blog, Facebook, YouTube, Flickr, and LinkedIn a little but it tends to be too dry for me."

12). What do you think your future with Twitter will be?
"Continue to make friends. That's what it's all about. Engage with people. It is people that make the difference."

Chapter 6 – Virtual Reality: Social Networking Warnings

"He who rejects change is the architect of decay. The only human institution which rejects progress is the cemetery."
– *Harold Wilson*

1. Shock of the New

On September 15th, 1830, the Liverpool and Manchester Railway opened in the Northwest of England, linking those two great cities. At the time, it was a truly amazing piece of the most modern technology available. Until that day, traveling the approximately 40 miles from city to city by stagecoach would take about six hours. However, on that world-changing day, freight and passengers could move along the track, and cover the distance in around two hours. Within a few years this was reduced further to just one hour. This meant that a train could make the journey up to five times for each stagecoach trip. In addition, the largest stagecoaches could carry ten passengers, with a crew of two and a team of 4 – 6 horses. One train, with its crew of 2, could carry 100 passengers. This meant that transportation efficiency was improved by 5,000 fold by the opening of the track. The cost of a stagecoach journey between the two cities was 16 shillings (almost a week's wages for a skilled man). By

1831, the fare for the same journey by train was only seven shillings putting the journey within reach of more people. This was a marvel of the early 19th century.

However, not everyone viewed the wonder as a good thing, and took every opportunity they could to dismiss it. On the opening day, to the delight of the detractors, there was a tragic accident. The Right Honourable William Huskisson, M.P., one of the most avid supporters of the railway, was injured when he was caught between two of the trains. The accident happened right in front of the Prime Minister, the Duke of Wellington, who had shook Huskisson's hand only moments before. As a result of the severity of his wounds Huskisson died later that evening.

For the opponents of progress, it was all they could wish for. Reporters wrote articles in newspapers about the dangers of traveling by train. Medical experts were consulted on the dangers to the human physique of traveling faster than 30 miles per hour. The fear generated in women, children, and livestock was a constant concern.

These 'lobbyists' from industries as diverse as blacksmiths, farmers, market owners, horse breeders, and of course stagecoach operators banded together to spread the bad news. They encouraged dissent in the eyes of the public by spreading spurious stories and tales about the evil that would abound as the railways spread their grip on the land. The ultimate culmination was several laws from the 1830s until the mid-1860s designed to reduce or eliminate the advantages of all steam powered vehicles.

Sound familiar? When a new technology is introduced, those with vested interests contrary to the progress, or those just plain scared of change, will do everything they can to discredit the new technology. All you have to do is to look at the history of almost anything that we currently take for granted. (I have a very amusing book that my dad bought in 1973 called "The Computer Survival Handbook" that guides you in avoiding or at least dealing with computers! And this was ten years before the IBM PC showed up!) You will often find many people opposing development and introduction to the masses of any significant invention. And so it is with Social Media and the Social Networking applications that support it.

Today's 'stagecoach operators and horse breeders' are a diverse bunch. Everything from traditional journalists, publishers, and marketers, to people who are involved directly in the web itself – web designers, web marketers, and especially 'SEO specialists' (SEO is Search Engine Optimization. It is the 'art' of pushing your online information to the top of search engine lists such as Google, Yahoo!, etc). They have a lot to loose as social media / networking takes hold. Websites and designs were the 'high art' of the internet. Good websites and high quality design are still very important, but social networking has (and will) provide a wider and more dynamic range of choices in these fields. And as far a SEO is concerned, social networking is becoming a big threat to this model of business marketing. After all, wouldn't you want to buy from someone or somewhere your friends and trusted partners already buy from? A social network of your contacts can tell you that. A Google search cannot.

Let me clarify that not all journalists, publishers, etc. are opposed to new technology, as I'm sure some stagecoach operators were forward thinking as well. It's just that some have been very vocal in their opposition. Be careful when listening to a salesman (and don't forget I'm selling YOU on the concepts of social networking here in this book ☺).

I must admit to being a "historical technologist." History has always fascinated me as much as the new. I believe in pushing the boundaries of knowledge and endeavor while remembering where we came from and what got us here in the first place. It is interesting (to me at least) how my own social networking experience has reflected this. I have not dropped going to plays (several thousand year old technology), reading books (almost 500 years old), watching movies at the cinema (100 years old), TV (1930's), or using Google to search for stuff (started January 1996). In marketing terms, trade shows, public presentations, advertising, PR, and various other forms of traditional tools still have a place in a solid marketing strategy. Social networking is just the "new thing" in the ever changing marketing mix. But it is here. And here it will stay.

I have a word of caution about the 'new' as it relates to which social networks you should align with and focus on. The 'new' gets old faster than ever before. In 2001, I got involved on a social network aimed at connecting former school friends. It was great. It filled the desire for people to get in touch with old school friends (yes, some people love that, and some people despise it… I'm making no judgment here). I signed up for one year and paid about $30 to get full access. I got in touch with a handful of people. We shared a couple of site entries, and I actually spoke to a few on the phone. However, due to its very narrow focus, and little to say after "hi, how are you?" my interest in the site waned.

Then along came Facebook. Because Facebook can be what you make it, and you can invite people to connect with you who you want to be connected with it is far more dynamic then the 'school friends' sites. I'm connected to old school friends I have not seen in 30 years, and I find it fascinating to see what has happened to people from my childhood.

2. Where you go on the web

I'm a dazzling urbanite, down home country boy at heart. I was raised in a moderate sized town half way between Manchester and Liverpool (and yes, the town had two stations on the original L&M railway!!). The town was directly to the west, east, and south of our house. To the north (at the back of our house) were two miles of gently rolling fields. I had the best of both worlds. For almost as long as I lived in that house I'd take first Sam (our black Labrador) and later Jenny (our Golden Retriever) for long hikes through the fields, having numerous adventures in that carefree piece of the planet. But the country boy had to give in to the urbanite once I came home through the back door of our house.

Growing up, until the age of 11 years old, I mixed with three main social networks:

1. My school pals
2. My cousins
3. The children of my parents friends

Each network served a purpose, even though I did not realize it then. On rare occasions, people from each network would mix together via my or my parent's invitation. The main networking events of my childhood were birthdays and Christmas. Fun, fun, fun...

At age 11, I went to high school. I know that is an alien concept for the average American reader. England in the mid-70s had a very different schooling structure (and content) from U.S. schools of the 90s and 2000s. For whatever reason, my parents decided to send us not to our local high school, but to one that was TWO towns away from where we lived. It took 1.5 hours each direction (on two or three public transport buses) to get to school and back. As a result, my grade school network dried up almost at once. My high school network was always hampered by these travel restraints. I knew many people at school, but I was only close to a few. These were the kids as determined as I was to spend time together on a weekend.

By the time I was 16, I regularly caught the bus(es) to visit my cousins, who lived about 30 miles away. A 2–3 hour ordeal was well worth a blissful 2–3 day weekend. I grew closer to my cousins in Southport than I did to my own siblings.

Manchester and Liverpool, being such large cities, and so close together, can cause problems. Crime of all forms infected different parts of the cities to different degrees. I saw people from my high school get sucked into these dangerous and potentially deadly networks. I distanced myself from anyone who was headed down those wrong paths. It wasn't a moral question; it was more self preservation on my part. The safety and security of my three networks at age ten had been blown apart. In less than a year, the influx of new and challenging social networks had changed everything for me.

The virtual world of the social network is constantly expanding. There are literally thousands to choose from. You should carefully select the social networks that you belong to. Here are three example criteria for selecting the networks.

First, is it something that interests you? This may sound obvious, but it's something you should think about. You can get overwhelmed with social networks if you are not careful. For example, I'm not interested in knitting. Therefore, I would not join The Knitting Guild Association (www.tkga.com just in case you are interested (a very nice looking site BTW)). However, I am interested in business connections in and around Metro Detroit, and therefore, I am a member of Motor City Connect (www.motorcityconnect.com if you are interested in that!). Stick to what you enjoy.

Second, can you contribute to the network? The only way you are going benefit from a social network is by giving something first. Imagine if you stood in a room of a hundred strangers in a hotel lobby and you need to find the elevator to go to your room. Nothing is going to happen until you ask someone for help. Don't be shy. Remember, when it comes to social networking, you are simply an e-mail address and user name. So start a conversation and see what happens.

Third, what is the benefit in joining the network? If you're interested in the subject of the network, you may think that you'll always benefit from it. But that is not always the case. The benefits are found by lively and involved members of the network. That is what makes the networks thrive and grow, and increases the value to the membership. Have a look around to make sure that something is going on there before you sign up (new networks and groups are important too, but just use some judgment).

And a word of caution!!! DO NOT SIGN UP WITH (or even visit) ANY GROUP OR NETWORK THAT MAY BE OF HARM TO YOU. Use common sense when you are surfing, looking, and joining!

3. Who is in your network

The rules of virtual social networking are very similar to traditional networking. You are known by the company you keep. But the virtual world *can* be tricky.

This is the obvious message that has been out as long as the World Wide Web: people can and do anything they want if you cannot see them. So ALWAYS use caution when dealing with any entity you have never met.

Although I am what is called an "open networker" in the terms of internet social networking, I'm not a dilettante when it comes to my privacy and the "inner me". I have some strong beliefs about the warnings associated with social networking. I take some seriously and others I choose to ignore. The best example of this is the way I handle my contact lists on Twitter, LinkedIn, and Facebook. I handle them in three distinct ways (*and remember, this is just the way I do it.* You may decide differently).

One key tenet of marketing is to get your name out to as wide an audience as possible, and let that audience know what you can do to help them. I have worked in sales and marketing for almost 25 years. To me, Twitter is (for now at least) the preeminent marketing tool in the social media arena. Even though it has a fraction of the users that networks such as Facebook and MySpace have, Twitter has three key ingredients that make it different: it is:

1. Fast
2. Simple
3. Direct

Effective marketing extends your message far and wide and as such I encourage as many Tweeps as possible to follow me. I check and verify all my follows before I decide to follow them. Twitter has made a great effort in keeping Tweeps from doing anything to upset the community. I have had followers disappear before I have had chance to check them out for following! While this is rare, I am very pleased to see it. This proves to me that Twitter is concerned about keeping its network clean, strong, and secure. In the simplest terms, on Twitter, I allow anyone to follow me, and I'll follow anyone who interests me.

Since this is 'The Twitter Workbook', let me diverge briefly and state my policies on LinkedIn and Facebook.

LinkedIn is labeled as a professional social network. I use it for marketing and business intelligence. With it, I have the most open policy of connecting to people. Three simple reasons: First, the more connections I have, the further my name gets out. Second, it broadens my view of the business world. Third, it makes it far easier to get information and help when I need it. Ask me sometime how I more than doubled my LinkedIn network in five days!

Facebook has my strictest requirements to be on my contact list. There are only two ways I'll add someone to my list in Facebook. Either I have met the person or someone I know and trust has met the person I'm connecting with. Facebook contains the most variety of uses of the three major applications I use, and has a lot of information about a lot of people on it. So it is here that I use the most caution.

Back to Twitter! When you first start using it, select a few people that you know to follow. Also do some searching to find people with common interests. By searching for certain keywords and phrases within Twitter you will find a wide variety of Tweeps to follow. Once you are following some Tweeps, enter into or start conversations that you find interesting. This will help you get the most out of your time on Twitter.

4. What you say on the web

Be careful of what you say and where and who you say it to. On December 30th, 2008, two of my good friends from Motor City Connect (mentioned above), Terry Bean and Charlie Wollborg, presented a workshop on goal setting in Troy, MI. During the presentation, Terry said "What goes on the internet stays on Google!" (Terry attributes the quote to Scott Monty (@ScottMonty)). That is so true! The internet is ever expanding and ever encompassing. And the spoken and written word (together with pictures and videos) has a serious habit of ending up on it.

One thing you should do on a regular basis is "Google yourself". Go to www.google.com and type in your name into the search field. If you have a very common name, you may have to add more information, like your home town or address to get results. In my case, I have to add my middle initial. As of today (mid-March, 2009) I have nine out of ten references on Google for David R Haslam. Not too bad I think. However, of more interest is what they tell you about me and what I have typed onto the internet. The first two listings are references to my LinkedIn account, next is a reference to Facebook, the following two are Twitter posts, etc. They are a clear indication of my online activity within my three main network applications. Googling DavidRHaslam yields lots of Tweets from your truly!

People will get an impression of you from what they see on the net. Correct or false, good, bad, or ugly, others will form an opinion. Therefore you should make sure that you stand by your words, and can handle others opinions if they are contrary to yours.

Positive attitude attracts positive people. And I like being associated with positive people. It is very rare that you will see me complain about ANYTHING on line, especially on Twitter. The last time I remember doing that was complaining about a political figure's view of what was happening in January 2008. Almost immediately two of the Tweeps that were following me leapt up to the defense of the figure. Wow! I was amazed, but also pleased. It shows how interactive Twitter can be. My best advice comes straight from the little rabbit, Thumper, in the classic Disney movie 'Bambi', and I quote "If you can't say something nice… don't say nothing at all." Online at least ☺

On Twitter, people will follow you based on what you say. Tweet about the subjects that interest you. Use words that you know that your peers use. For example, if you are a Toastmaster, words and phrases like Club, Area, Division, District, CC, CL, ACB, ACS, TLI etc will be known to you and any other Toastmaster would understand those references. If you like knitting, use knitting terminology in your Tweets. By talking about the things that interest you, people will start communicating on those subjects in return.

5. *What you CANNOT say on the web*

Information disclosure, secrecy, privacy, and ethical standards are all key elements in modern life. While social networking seems to be one, big free-for-all of communication, there are some limits. You should be aware of both personal and professional confines that you have to work within.

False information about and verbal attacks on others can be the worst thing you can do in the virtual world. Others can rapidly develop a negative impression of you which may be hard to shake. People will not want to listen to you after a while. You also run the risk of making a libelous statement that could land you in trouble with the law. Always remember Thumper's advice!

Some professions have severe restrictions on information disclosure. Medical, finance, defense, and various arms of the government are a few examples. If you have *any restrictions* on use of data within your organization, it may affect the virtual world as well. Before you setup ANY social network account, you should check with your HR department if you have any doubt.

Other professions have very strict ethical and behavioral expectations. While some jobs may have these defined in employee manuals, others may not. Teaching is probably the best example of how ethics and behavior can have a strong influence on work. If you are unsure of how to apply this to the virtual world, just use your real world rules.

Privacy is another major concern. You can talk as much or as little as you want about things that are private to you. However, NEVER share private information about an organization or individual unless you have their permission or THEY have already released it in public. (And you have to be careful about the circumstances as well.) Some organizations are very open and public, and yet they still have 'classified' events or data. Keep it that way!

In general, if you have ANY doubts about sending a particular Tweet, just don't send it.

Case Study 6 – Not For Profit

"If you wish to experience peace, provide peace for another."
- *Tenzin Gyasto, The 14th Dalai Lama*

Twitter has some amazing potential for fundraising / non-profit use. A key piece of advice is to *talk about yourself* in a very broad sense on Twitter. Talk about work, family, leisure, but also any non-profit activities that you do. You may see the rewards of this very quickly!

Rotary International is a large and established non-profit service organization. I belong to the Rotary Club of Plymouth a.m. (and not the Rotary Club of Plymouth...). The club meets at 7:00 a.m. on Tuesday mornings, which makes the meetings challenging for a night owl like me. In October 2008, I Tweeted about our meeting. We had discussed plans to setup a Miracle League baseball field in Plymouth. I thought that was interesting enough to Tweet about.

Within minutes, I was followed by @CaryRotaryClub. I returned the favor. After many interesting conversations about Rotary and non-profit activities in general, I decided to contact the person behind the Tweep. The first time I spoke to Andy Wright (aka @CaryRotaryClub) was to build this case study. The story he had to tell was quite amazing! The power of Twitter strikes again!

1). Twitter ID:
   @CaryRotaryClub
   @Andy_Wright

2). Personal or professional use:
   "I use Twitter predominately for professional use, as in the Cary-Kildaire Rotary Club (non-profit). But I also use my other account for some personal stuff."

3). Did you try anything similar before Twitter?
   "I've been on Facebook for over three years and still maintain a presence there. I was almost forced into it. A lot of kids in our church youth group used Facebook and as a youth group councilor they started sending me invites to join. My son, who at the time was 16 years old was on it too and was getting into the dating scene. As a parent, it gave some added benefits on keeping tabs on him! It's worked out well."

4). Who introduced you to it?
   "I found Twitter through research. With 28 years in sales and marketing and 19 years at IBM, I always try to keep on top of marketing and tech trends. @TwiterMaven had a blog post about Twitter branding. I was first looking at it for my company, Global Knowledge, and realized how I could use it for Cary-Kildaire Rotary Club. I found @Rotary on Twitter in October 2008. Cary-Kildaire Rotary Club became one of the first three clubs to make use of it. Now, there are over 60 clubs using Twitter."

5). When did you start?
   "October / November 2008"

6). Why do you use Twitter?

"I mainly use it to promote Rotary to Rotarians and non-Rotarians. I try to reach out to people who are interested in helping others. It promotes the Rotarian motto: 'Service above self'. It has been useful in attracting potential members in the local area. It has become a great way to reach out to a younger audience, and encourage different generations to look into the work of Rotary."

7). What do you Tweet about?

"I Tweet about several areas. The weekly Cary-Kildiare Rotary Club program is the main subject. Local and community oriented news also features in my Tweets. I re-Tweet @Rotary, and use <u>TwitterFeed</u> for stories from the Rotary International web site. <u>GoogleReader</u> with <u>FriendFeed</u> helps me to keep tabs on other information of a local interest. In terms of tools and applications I use Tweetdeck, <u>TweeterKharam</u>, <u>SocialToo</u>, and <u>TweetPic</u> to enhance my Twitter experience."

8). Any advice that you would like to share?

"Think twice before you Tweet. (Employers may be reading, so be very careful what you say). Always remove your emotion from Twitter. If you are using Twitter for a non-profit, be extra careful. DO NOT BE CONTREVERSAL. Also, don't be someone you are not. People tend to be more sophisticated on Twitter. Always avoid SPAM. Use good etiquette. Follow your followers."

9). Your best Twitter experience?

"In February of 2009, as Webmaster of our club website, I received an email plea for help. It came from a woman in New Hampshire whose best friend's daughter was tragically injured in a farming accident in Candor, North Carolina. While auguring holes to plant peach trees, Katie Parson's clothing got tangled in the augur and she sustained severe injuries to her body. Katie was airlifted to UNC Children's Hospital in Chapel Hill, NC. The family had limited resources and no insurance. The woman didn't know who to turn to for help in North Carolina. She had sent the email to the first Rotary Club she came across in a Google search (our club), some 4H Clubs, Future Farmers of America organizations and a few other non-profits. Our Rotary Club was the only one to reply back to her. Our club quickly organized with other local Rotary Clubs in our District (7710) to help the family find housing in Chapel Hill while Katie was hospitalized, and to provide food and other essentials for the family during their stay. I started Tweeting about the tragedy, needs that the family had at the time, and about a fund established at a local bank for donations for the family. Through Tweeter, we received an incredible outpouring of love, support, encouragement and financially support. Soon, blogs and Facebook pages were started to spread the word. It restored my faith in the goodness of strangers."

10).   Top three Tweeps that you would recommend?
"Depends on what you are looking for or interested in
         @RichardBranson
         @JohnCleese
         @CaryRotaryClub !"

11).   Other social networks you use regularly?
"Mainly, YouTube and Facebook."

12).   What do you think your future with Twitter will be?
         "First, the Rotarian part of me would say more Rotary involvement will be a good thing. There are current about 2,500 - 3,000 Rotarians involved on Twitter. As that number rises, we can leverage Twitter for national and international projects. Secondly, for my 'day job' use, I see it as a way to link local business and services to benefits

they can provide. For example, if I'm going to a new town for the first time, I can use Twitter to find local information and services that can help me. I like that."

Part 3 – How to Twitter?

"Teaching is more than imparting knowledge, it is inspiring change.
Learning is more than absorbing facts, it is acquiring understanding."
> - *William Arthur Ward*

Chapter 7 - Twitter Basics

"After 'Norwegian Wood', I met Ravi Shankar at a friend's house in London, for dinner. He offered to give me instructions in the basics of the sitar, like how to sit, how to hold it, and the basic exercises. It was the first time I had ever really learned these sort of things."
  - George Harrison

We are planning to update The Twitter Workbook each quarter. Things change very quickly these days. If what you see below does not match up to what you see on the Twitter web site please let us know. We recommend visiting www.HMSI-inc.com and registering your copy of the book.

1. Getting started – again!

As promised, this section takes a more in-depth look at setting up your account on Twitter. Let's get started again ☺.

1).   Make sure you have an e-mail account on which you do not mind getting SPAM. Not to accuse Twitter of spamming; it is just a good idea for virtual social networking in general.

E-mail Address:_____

2). Open your Internet browser of choice (Internet Explorer, Firefox, Opera, etc.)

3). Go to www.Twitter.com.

4). Click the 'Get Started – Join!' button at the lower center of the web page.

5). Enter the full name you would like to appear on your profile.

When choosing the full name, remember that it will be picked up by internet search engines (such as Google, Yahoo! etc.) Keep the same name for the same purpose on as many social networks as you can. Some people have multiple user accounts for different purposes. The most common approach is to use one Twitter account for professional use, and a second for personal. However, if you have multiple professional uses, there is nothing restricting you from using more the two accounts. Keeping a consistent name will help to improve your search engine optimization (SEO).

Name:_____

Full name   **Twitt Workbook**   ✔ ok

6). Enter your user name. (Letters and numbers only. No spaces or special characters). Treat the user name with the same importance as the full name. Make sure they are consistent with each other, as well as consistent with the purpose of your account.

User Name:_____

Username   **TwittWorkbook**   ✔ ok

7). Enter your password. Use a password that is easy for you to remember, but difficult for others to figure out. Include numbers and capitalization to make it tough for the hackers.

Password:_____

Password ••••••••• ✔ Good

8). Enter your e-mail address mentioned above.

Email twittbook@comcast.net ✔ ok

9). Click on the box if you want the inside scoop. You may always unsubscribe later.

☐ I want the inside scoop—please send me email updates!

10). Type in the "anti-bot" words shown on the screen. With the rise of SPAM and spyware, membership web sites have been fighting back. They routinely have methods of preventing automated programs ("bots") from logging in. Below is Twitter's.

11). Click the "Create My Account" button.

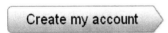

12). The next screen is 'See if your friends are on Twitter'. You can either click 'Skip this step' at the bottom, or follow the steps below.

12a). The page allows you to search YOUR address book on five major e-mail systems.

See if your friends are on Twitter

12b). Once you click on the network of choice, the page changes, allowing you to enter information to conduct the search. Type in your e-mail address and password for the network, and click 'Continue'.

Note the dates when you checked your e-mail networks (you'll thank me later):

Gmail: ____/____/____   ____/____/____
Yahoo: ____/____/____   ____/____/____
AOL: ____/____/____   ____/____/____
Hotmail: ____/____/____   ____/____/____
MSN: ____/____/____   ____/____/____

12c). The page will change again to let you know that it is processing data. Just wait.

Contacting Yahoo...

We're loading your contacts.
(This can take a while if you've got a large address book.)

12d). All the contacts in your address book will be listed. *Make sure that you un-select all your contacts first.* You may have people in your address book that you no longer want to contact! Once you have done that, select the contacts you want to inform about your ID on Twitter. I've edited my list below to protect the innocent!

12e). When you click Invite, Twitter sends an e-mail to the contacts, inviting them to the Twitterverse.

Note the people you have invited:

_____

_____

_____

_____
_____
_____
_____
_____
_____
_____

13).   And the final screen is 'Look who else is here. Start following them!' These are famous / infamous Tweeps. Click on any that you might be interested in. Click the "Finish" button, or the 'Skip this step' link as you like.

14).   Type in "Greetings! I'm finally on Twitter! #TTWB", and click "update". You have just sent your first Tweet!   Congratulations!!!   You are now part of the Twitterverse! Note: #TTWB is called a hash-tag. These are used to ease searching for Tweets at some future point, or to track activity related to a particular subject. In this case, TTWB stands for "The Twitter Workbook".

2. Twitter home page

They say that *home is where the heart is!* On any website, the heart is where the home page is. The Twitter home page is one of the simplest around. Let's take a look.

1). Open your Internet browser of choice.

2). Use the browser to go to www.Twitter.com.

3). Unless you are Japanese, ignore the Select Language option. If you are Japanese, click on the drop down arrow, and select the Japanese language. (If you want to try it anyway, go ahead. You can easily switch back to English).

Select Language ... ▼	Tried it:___/___/_____

4). If you haven't already tried, click the Watch a video! button. It is amusing, but I must say, a little bit dated (yes, March 2008 is dated by internet standards!). Read the first half of the next chapter to find out more about reasons and ways to use Twitter effectively.

▶ Watch a video!	Watched it:___/___/_____

5). The three buttons in the middle of the Twitter home page try to tell you more about reasons for Twitter. Again, in my opinion, it is somewhat dated advice. They may have been what Twitter intended users to do, but that is not what has happened...

What?	Why?	How?	Clicked it:___/___/____

6).   Next is the login panel.   Enter your username or e-mail address (as you recorded in Chapter 2 - Quick Start), followed by your password, and then click the *Sign In* button.   If you want Twitter to remember your sign in information, click on the *Remember me* check box.   If you have forgotten your password, click the *Click here* link.

Please sign in

user name or email address:

password:

☐ Remember me   Sign In »

Forgot password? Click here.

7).   If you have been using Twitter from your cell phone, click the *Click here* link in the green box.

Already using Twitter from
your phone? Click here.

8).   At the bottom of the home page is a menu bar. About Us, Contact, and Blog are all standard features of most web sites.   In brief, *About Us* explains a history of Twitter, and describes more about the people who run the organization.   It also includes the links to reach all the employees of Twitter using Twitter! *Contact* gives address information to reach Twitter by "snail mail".   *Blog* links you to an amusing and thorough blog of company activities. The blog page also contains other useful links.

About Us   Contact   Blog

9). The *Status* link is used by Twitter to report any issues that they have had with the operational status of the Twitter application itself. If you have had problems with Twitter, this is a good place to check if it was not YOUR problem ☺

Status

10). The *Apps* link takes you to a page that displays twelve applications that are designed to work with Twitter.

Apps

11). Twitter has a great API (application programming interface), however, most Twitter users will never be interested in it. An API is used by programmers to exchange information between different computer applications. One reason Twitter has become so popular among the "worldwide web geeks" is that it offers a good, free API. If you are really THAT interested in it, click the link and have fun! ☺

API

12). *Search* and *Help* are two more common links on a lot of web sites. The search capability adds amazing power to Twitter. You can add a word or phrase to the search and find out who is talking about anything with that word or phrase. *Help* gives you more in depth help on Twitter. Just like most computer users with most manuals, most people I know have never looked at it. However, there is a vast amount of information on the page. I'd say the most critical for getting help, would be the five members of Twitter Support who have their Twitter address on the opening paragraph, and the e-mail address for support, listed here for your convenience: support@twitter.com

Search Help

15).   The final elements on the home page are *Terms* and *Privacy*. Again, these are fairly standard on many social network sites. My advice is read them if it concerns you. In other words, if you feel that you are going to push the limits of normal industry terms of use, or you are going to put things on Twitter that you are nervous about keeping private, or giving away your e-mail address etc., ***read them!***

Terms Privacy

3. Your home page

Once you login to Twitter, you will be directed to your own personal home page. This is your working hub in your own Twitterverse. Let's explore!

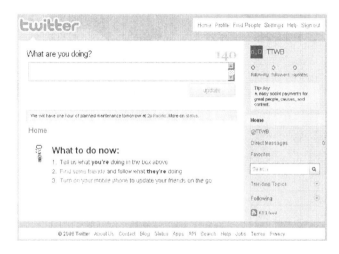

1). The Twitter logo at the top left of the page acts as a refresh button. If you click it, the page will be refreshed and reloaded.

2). *Home* works exactly the same way as the Twitter logo.

3). An important part of your long time use of Twitter is to setup an effective profile. You set it up by clicking the *Profile* link.

Profile

4). Use the *Find People* link to do just that, find people you are looking for ☺.

Find People

5). *Settings* allows you to setup all the details of your account. This is another important element to improve your Twitter experience.

Settings

6). To get help on your home page, click the *Help* link. (It links to the same help page referenced above).

Help

7). The *Sign out* link, will take you back to the Twitter home page and allow you to sign back in with a different account.

Sign out

8). The main, central function of Twitter is right (or write ☺) here. In the box under *What are you doing?*, you are expected to write about the stuff you are up to at that minute. But it is so much more than just that. As I've said before, Twitter is a very powerful tool. Tweeps enter all sorts of information. Just get involved, take a look, and see what I mean.

As you enter text in the box, the gray number will tell you how many characters that you have left. When you get to 19 to 10 characters left, the number will turn maroon. At nine and below, it will turn red. If you go below 0 you'll see a negative number, in which case Twitter will not allow you to send your message. Either re-write your message, or use some abbreviations to shorten it. (Use & in place of 'and', 1st for first, nite for good night, etc.) Once you are happy with your Tweet, click the update button to send it out to the Twitterverse (or at least your followers).

Posted just below the box, in gray text, is the last Tweet you sent. This helps you track your portion of conversations you are in, or what was last on your mind to Twitter about.

9). The next portion of the page is all about you! If you click the *Profile* link (listed above) or your picture your public profile will appear. (Until you upload a picture, it will be a small brown square with a blue design on it). This is what the rest of the Twitterverse gets to see; information about you. If you plan on expanding your Twitter-based network beyond the people that you already know, it is very important to create an interesting and honest profile.

Your profile will help people determine if they want to follow you.

To create or edit your profile, click the *Settings* link. The Settings page provides all the tools that you need to create a great profile.

Three critical numbers in Twitter are:

1. How many people you are following
2. How many people are following you
3. How many updates (or Tweets) you have sent out

The three links shown will take you to more detailed information on these subjects. Each of the three pages will be looked into later.

10). The box directly below is a recent addition to Twitter. It changes periodically when you log in or update the home page. In effect, it is advertising either additional Twitter features, or third party software. Some examples are shown below:

11). Occasionally, Twitter will display a warning message that they are performing updates. Click on *service* if you are concerned about an interruption of service during that time. It will give you more details. Below is a typical warning message:

We will have one hour of planned maintenance tomorrow at 2p Pacific. More on status.

12). The center and main portion of the page is taken up with recent Tweets from *YOU AND THE PEOPLE YOU FOLLOW*. *This is key*. If you do not follow someone, you will not see their Tweets. When you first set up Twitter (or if you are not following anyone), this section will look like this:

Home

What to do now:

1. Tell us what **you're** doing in the box above
2. Find some friends and follow what **they're** doing
3. Turn on your mobile phone to update your friends on the go

Once you start following other people, this section will updated each time you refresh the web page. Here is a selection of some of the people that I follow and how they would appear in the center section:

13). On the right side of the page are a series of tabs. The *Home* tab is the first, and it displays the current page you are on, *your Home page*!

14). The second tab is *@Replies* (it will display as *@your user name*). This displays all the replies that people have sent back to you. A reply (or just a reference) starts with the @ symbol.

15). People whom you follow can also send *Direct Messages*. These are private between you and the sender (just like e-mail). Caution: do not send "just anything". Remember Mr. Bean's words from the previous chapter *"What goes on the internet..."*

16). If you really like a Tweet, that someone you are following has sent, then you can mark for your *Favorites* folder. You access these older Tweets using the *Favorites* tab.

17). The section of the page that shows a set of thumbnail pictures lets other people see some of the Tweeps that you are following. If you put your mouse pointer over a thumb nail, a "smart tag" will display the name and Twitter address of your contact. People also have the option of looking at all your Tweeps by clicking *View All...* YOU can also click the *add* link to make additions to your Tweeps.

18). The *RSS feed* link allows you to add Tweets to whatever RSS system that you have setup. (See http://en.wikipedia.org/wiki/RSS_(protocol) if you would like more information.)

19). Clicking the *More* button shows you addition Tweets that Tweeps have sent...

4. Find People

The *Find People* page has recently been changed and much improved. You are lucky if you never used the old one. There are four tabs that you can use:

1). The *Find on Twitter* tab is the first. It is very straight forward. Just type in a username, or first or last name of someone that you are looking for. In this example, let's try Haslam.

Press the Enter key or click the *search* button. The results (at least the first two) are below...

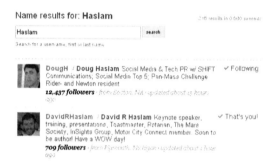

To look at the person's profile, click on the photo or user name. Or just click on the *Follow* button to start following them.

2). The *Find on other networks* tab allows you to search YOUR address book on five major e-mail systems.

Once you click on the network of choice, the tab changes, allowing you to enter information to search.

All the contacts in your address book will be listed. CAUTION: The default is that all of the contacts will be selected. DO NOT just click *Follow*. To deselect all of them, click the check box next to *Select All*.

When you agree with the selections, click *Follow.* You will then be given the opportunity to invite people in your address book. Again, use caution, or you will invite everyone else in your address book. *I've edited the list below to protect the innocent!*

None of your contacts are on Twitter. Want to invite some?

These people are in your address book, but aren't on Twitter yet. We can send invites to the contacts you select below. See what you'll send them.

When you click *Invite*, Twitter sends an e-mail to the contacts, inviting them to the Twitterverse.

3). *Invite by e-mail* allows you to invite ANYONE with an e-mail account that you know. Fill in the e-mail addresses, separated by commas, and click the Invite.

When you send an invitation, this is what the e-mail will look like.

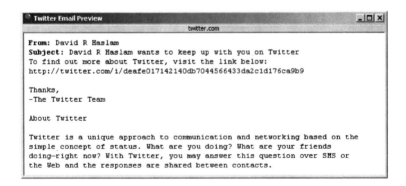

4). The fourth and final tab is *Suggested Users*. It is a list of interesting and eclectic current Twitter users. Scroll through the list, and click on the check box next to anyone who interests you. A thumbnail image will be added under *You will be following*. When you are happy with your selections, click the *Follow* button. Twitter will then return to your home page, and briefly display a banner telling you how many new people you are following.

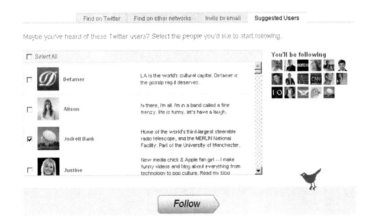

5. Search

Searching on Twitter is one of the best things about it. You can find people that have similar interests to you. From beginners to experts, or just casual observers. Let's try something:

1). Make sure you are logged into your home page on Twitter.

2). As an example, type "Ticket to ride" in the Search field:

3).   Press *Enter* or click the magnifying glass. Wonder what we'll see?

4).   Your results will be undoubtedly different to example below, however, an explanation of these results will help:

5).   The panel shows the search results on all the Tweets that are out there. To demonstrate the results, I added one myself. My picture and user name (in blue) are shown at the top. With any of the results listed, you can click on either the picture or the user name to see the user profile. Within the text of the Tweet, all words associated with the search will be in **bold.** Only Tweets that include all the words from your search are shown. If you want an exact phrase, enclose it in quotation marks: "ticket to ride".

6).   You can also save your searches for later use. Click *Save this search.*

⊕ Save this search

Once you save your search, you will see it listed just below the search box:

Also, you will be given the option to remove the search:

⊗ Remove this saved search

6. Profile

Access your own profile by clicking the *Profile* link at the top of your home page.

To see profiles of other people, click on their name or picture from updates, search results, or follower lists. Below is the profile of @EleART:

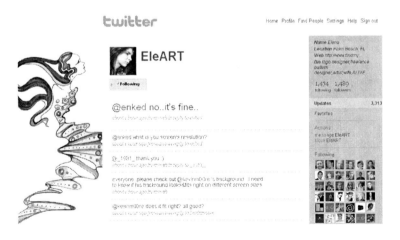

The information block contains the name (very important for *search engine optimization (SEO)* that was covered in section 1 of this chapter), location, a web site address, and some biographical information. (All these items are created on the *Settings* page covered in the next section).

You can look at a chronological list of the person's *Updates*, as well as Tweets that they have flagged as *Favorites*. By default, the *Updates* are displayed. Simply click on *Updates* or *Favorites* to switch between the two lists.

You can send a *Direct Message* (or DM in Twitter language, see below for details) or block a user using *Actions*. You can only block someone that you are not following. When you block them, they will not see anymore of your updates.

If you click the 'block' link, you will see a warning page. Read it carefully before committing to the block. Once you are sure what you want to do, click the appropriate button.

7. Settings

The heart of setting up your Twitter account is the *Settings* page. The page has six tabs.

Account

The base tab contains the details as follows:

1).   The *Name* is your Full Name entered during your sign up on Twitter.

2).   *Username* was also entered during your sign up.

3).   *E-mail* is the address you entered during your sign up...

If your e-mail address is not valid, or becomes in active, Twitter will display this message on your home page. When you click the link, you will go to the *Settings* page.

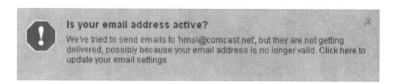

Is your email address active?

We've tried to send emails to 'hmsi@comcast.net', but they are not getting delivered, possibly because your email address is no longer valid. Click here to update your email settings

4). Select your *Time Zone* from the drop down list. All the U.S. time zones (and Canadian ones that match) are at the top of the list.

Time Zone: (GMT-05:00) Eastern Time (US & Canada)

5). Add the URL of you website for people to find out more about you. This is very important if you are using Twitter professionally or on behalf of another organization. The URL is a great way to directly link your Twitter activities to your brand.

More Info URL:

Have a homepage or a blog? Put the address here.
(You can also add Twitter to your site here)

6). Click the link to get help adding Twitter to a variety of other sites including MySpace, Facebook, and even your own website.

(You can also add Twitter to your site here)

7). The *One Line Bio* will be displayed on your profile. This is a great way for people to find out more about you... quickly! Be concise and accurate, *and be sure to check it for spelling and grammar.* Also, check how the bio looks on your profile. You can change it any time.

One Line Bio:

About yourself in fewer than 160 chars.

8). *Where in the world are you?* This has a little irony, since Twitter is a global social network. But it may be of interest for others who want to connect with you. If all else fails, *Earth* works fine, it's just not very helpful!

Location:

Where in the world are you?

9). The *Language* option allows you to set how you want to "speak" on Twitter. Yes, right now the choices are rather limited.

Language: English

What language would you like to Twitter in?

10). Click the *Protect My Updates* if you want to restrict your Tweets to a qualified group on the Twitterverse. With this option checked, you must approve all your followers before they can see what you have Tweeted about. You can always change this setting if you are not happy with your current privacy.

☐ Protect my updates

Only let people whom I approve follow my updates. If this is checked, you WILL NOT be on the public timeline. Updates posted previously may still be publicly visible in some places.

The *public timeline* link shows you *all* Tweets that are posted and are NOT private. This can be very useful when you are first starting to use Twitter. You can quickly see the immense diversity of people and subjects that are active on Twitter.

public timeline.

11). Click the *Save* button when you have completed all your changes.

Save

12). If you want to permanently delete your Twitter account, click the *Delete my account* link.

Delete my account.

If you click the link, a warning page is displayed. **Read it carefully.** Think twice before you click the *OKAY, FINE, DELETE MY ACCOUNT* button. If you do click that button, we will be sorry to see you go!

Password

The *Password* tab allows you to change your password at any time. Password security is always very important and was covered earlier n this book.

Devices

The *Devices* tab allows you to setup a mobile device for Twitter. Using a mobile device adds a whole new dimension to Twitter. If you text a lot of the time, you may find that Twitter enhances your capabilities to communicate easily, flexibly, and powerfully. Try it and see. Once you setup your mobile device, you can send general Tweets, as well as *Direct Messages*. You will also get incoming *Direct Messages*. You may select to receive Tweets only from certain people on your mobile device. This will be covered in the section below on *Followers*.

Enter your mobile number (don't forget to use a "+", or it will not work!), check the *'It's okay for Twitter to...'* box, and click *Save*.

You will now be asked to verify your setup. (You can only set this up for a phone you can actually put your hands on). Note the code to text to a number. This is to verify the correct setup. You can either send the text from your mobile device, or click the *Delete and start over?* button.

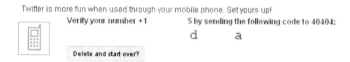

Twitter is more fun when used through your mobile phone. Set yours up!

Verify your number +1   5 by sending the following code to 40404:

d   a

Delete and start over?

Once you send the text from your mobile device, within seconds, you should get a reply. This means that you are now mobile with Twitter! Whole new vistas are waiting!

Notices

To quote the Twitter website, "These settings control much we bug you about various things." Let's break it done and look at each one of the four:

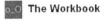 **The Workbook**

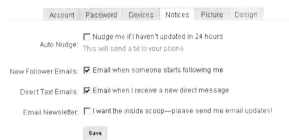

1).   The 'Auto Nudge' setting is especially useful if you are trying to build your brand / following using Twitter. If you have the setting checked, and you do not Tweet for 24 hours, you will get a message on your mobile device. *Make sure your mobile device is setup, otherwise this setting is useless.*

2).   If you have the *New Follower Emails* setting checked, each time someone decides to take an interest and follows you, you will automatically be informed. Again, this is great for newer users. To know that people are looking at your Tweets is a good thing and an affirmation that you are doing things right. It's also an opportunity to find more users to follow.

3).   A very useful setting is the *Direct Text Emails* setting. If you have checked the setting, each time a person *THAT YOU ARE FOLLOWING* sends you a *Direct Message,* a copy of that message will be sent to your e-mail. See below for a more detailed explanation *Direct Messages.*

4).   Checking the fourth setting, *Email Newsletter* signs you up for a periodic newsletter from Twitter.

Picture

This is where you to upload a picture to appear with your profile. When you click the '*Choose…*' button, a pop-up browse window opens. Select the picture you want to use (it needs to be smaller than 700kb). Click the *Open* button. Then click the *Save* button to see the picture take the place of that strange brown and blue impressionistic icon. Leaving that icon in place marks you as a newbie for many Tweeps. One person I know will not follow anyone who does not show a picture of themselves. It does help a lot when you attend a Tweet-Up because you will actually recognize people!

Design

Design is used to setup the background or wallpaper for your home page. You can choose from standard ones, or you can upload a custom design that you have created. Having a good background is a great way to show additional information. Advertise more about you or your organization. Make use of the space that Twitter gives you! It will help to generate interest in you.

Note: You can also add your own custom backgrounds. This will help raise you to a higher level. There are websites and people that can help you do this. If you are interested and would like more help, let me know!

8. Following

When you are looking at someone else's *Home Page*, on the right side, clicking on the *Following* link will show you who they are following. It will indicate if you are following them or not. If you want to start following them, click the *follow* button below their username.

9. Followers

To see a person's followers, click their *Followers* link. All the same features are present as with *Following*.

In the example below, you can see two additional features. <u>First</u>, the padlock 🔒 indicates that the Tweep has protected their updates. They have to grant you permission to allow you to follow them. <u>Second</u>, if you have a mobile device setup with Twitter, you can select if you want a persons updates to go to your phone or not Device updates: ○ On ⊙ Off.

10.　Updates

Clicking *Updates* takes you to the Tweep's home page and displays ONLY their updates in chronological order.

11.　@Replies

The @Replies link (it will display as *@your user name*) displays all the replies that people have sent back to you. A reply (or just a reference) starts with the @ symbol.

The page allows you to reply, or put in any Tweet you want. It is a great way of keeping track of what people are saying about you.

12. Direct Messages

Direct Messaging (DM) is totally private. It allows you to send a message to just one person. There are two tabs. The first is your *Inbox*, and the second is *Sent*.

To reply to or send another a direct message, move the mouse pointer over the message and click on the gray arrow ↖. Type in your reply, and click *Send*.

Case Study 7 – Bacon & The Bean

"Better beans and bacon in peace than cakes and ale in fear."
  - *Aesop*

Terry Bean and Charlie Wollborg have been mentioned a few times so far. These "partners-in-crime" run a group called Motor City Connect (MCC). Since 2007 it has grown to become a preeminent network for business people in Southeast Michigan. It operates in both real and virtual realms. As well as a very active online community (www.motorcityconnect.com), MCC also hosts MCC Live Events three days a week, regular educational seminars, rounded out by a range of social and networking occasions.

Terry and Charlie live the networking life. *They seem to be everywhere!* I've seen them at chamber of commerce events, Automation Alley, diversity groups, to name just a few. By making the network rounds, they have literally thousands of contacts. Passionate and positive, the create enthusiasm in others by their effervescing energy. This creates a magnetic effect. As a result, MCC has added over 3,000 members in about one year.

Terry himself is a caring and sharing person. Since the day I met him, he has shown that he cares about the people around him by sharing his time and wisdom and that is a fundamental principal of both real world and web based social networking: caring about the condition of others and sharing of yourself. That is the true secret to Terry's success. Here is what Terry has to say on the subject:

1). Twitter ID:
@TerryBean

2). Personal or professional use:
"There is no mainly personal or professional use. Both are intertwined. I don't distinguish between the two in Twitter"

3). Did you try anything similar before Twitter?
"Interesting question, there was nothing truly similar to Twitter before. But in terms of social networking, I joined LinkedIn in 2004, Plaxo and Facebook in 2006. I also used Yahoo groups at that time. I created Motor City Connect (MCC) on November 1, 2006, and it was officially launched on February 17, 2007."

4). Who introduced you to it?
"I was on a social media panel discussion at *Ann Arbor Spark!* in March 2008. Somebody (I think Ross Johnson) asked a very interesting social networking question. If Facebook and LinkedIn had a wrestling match and Twitter refereed, who would win? Lori Laurent Smith, Ed Vielmetti, and I were on the panel, and Derek Mehraban (@mehraban) was the moderator. Ed / Lori / Derek answered that Twitter would easily beat the other two. This was the first time I had heard of it. I signed up that month."

5). When did you start?
"March 25th 2008 according to http://whendidyoujointwitter.com/"

6). Why do you use Twitter?

"A handful of reasons. I use it to learn, give or receive help, promote people (myself, but mainly others) and *ask* (things I'm looking for, or things other people need). Also, I use it for the sheer entertainment value."

7). What do you Tweet about?

"I Tweet about interesting links, profound statements, other good people, and upcoming events. I also join in engaging conversations."

8). Any advice that you would like to share?

"First and foremost it should be fun and entertaining to do. Not stressful. If you are stressing out about what you Tweet or what you read, you should not be using it.

Second, it is good to learn *Twittiquette*. It helps to know when to re-Tweet (RT), direct message (DM), and when and where to use people's names.

Third, you should shine the light on others whenever you can. This is how social communities are built. It's not always about you or other people it is always about ALL OF US. Good networking.

And lastly, extend who you are. Twitter will not make you a rock star but extend your rock star ability. And it will not make you a jerk but may extend your jerk-ability. So think about how you would like to be known."

9). Your best Twitter experience?

"My best experience was... A few. One cool thing is that my auto-responder says "how can I make the day great for you". A guy was looking for a job for his girl-friend in the medical field. A couple of days before I had heard about a position through my network. I connected the two, and she interviewed for the medical job. Jay Brenfield asked about marketing "Twitter shock and awe". Bob Burg (who is an author and a kind of mentor to me) gave me two shout outs on #FollowFriday. I also saw my name next to Alyssa Milano on #FollowFriday. Now there is a case of beauty and the beast!"

10).   Top three Tweeps that you would recommend?
@CharlieCurve
@OneCoach
@DaveGlenn

11).   Other social networks you use regularly?
"80% of my social network time is spent on Facebook, Motor City Connect, LinkedIn, and Twitter. Plaxo, Collective X, and Ning groups make up most of the rest.

12).   What do you think your future with Twitter will be?
"Interesting. I'll stay engaged on Twitter as long as the people are engaging. As long as it stays good, I'll be there. With Oprah on board we will have to wait and see what happens. Maybe I'll move to a new place if Twitter looses its positive aspects. Twitter is a tool. Like any tool it will run its course, and may be replaced. I'm the same jackass on a business call, as on Twitter, as anything else. As more people are finding out about it, there is always the risk of it becoming filled with "internet trash". But it hasn't happened yet. And as far as the potential of internet privacy / stalking issues are concerned: this is an advantage of being a big, ugly male, right David?"

Within the circles of social networking (both real world and online) in Southeast Michigan, Charlie Wollborg is well known and liked. With a broad smile and bundle of energy, he spreads enthusiasm in his wake. As you will see, local business and community figure large in his thinking. However, he is not adverse to national and international concerns as well. In addition, Charlie is well known for his passion for bacon!

1).   Twitter ID:
        @CharlieCurve
        @CharlieWollborg

"A best practice suggestion is to have multiple Twitter accounts. While @CharlieCurve is my main account, I setup @CharlieWollborg so that if people are searching for my name, they'll find me. Twitter has a high abandonment of accounts [accounts that are setup, used for a short time, and then abandoned without being deleted]. Although Twitter does not remove these accounts at the moment, I Tweet occasionally from @CharlieWollborg to stop it being thought of as abandoned."

2).   Personal or corporate use:
        "I am an *AND* person. I do not use Twitter for *either / or*. I use it for *EVERYTHING*. I'm pro-Michigan to help grow our local economy. To do that, you must help to grow businesses and spread ideas. I take the stance of being a thought leader. I use one Twitter account for an integrated life. Sales people have conversations about non business stuff during meeting. I don't have a problem integrating the two online."

3).   Did you try anything similar before Twitter?
        "My job is about finding new things and technologies. I fell in love with Twitter at the start. Love

at first Tweet I guess. I've tried other Twitter-style things, but nothing compares. Twitter is still the best at what it does."

4). Who introduced you to it?
"One of the blogs or printed sources that I'm constantly reading. I'm not even sure to be honest."

5). When did you start?
"Just before Terry. I told him about it, and how awesome it is. Oct 28th, 2007. Interesting! 5555 Tweets as of this interview. I wonder if that is significant!"

6). Why do you use Twitter?
"I use it to promote business and expertise. It is networking to learn. Twitter is networking, university, promotion rolled into one. Still a useful tool even though it's become more main stream. Twitter has changed and evolved. People don't look at you like you are crazy when you say "I'm Tweeting"."

7). What do you Tweet about?
"Everything! Marketing wisdom. Funny, amusing, and interesting stuff. Fortune cookie wisdom! Local events. Fatherly advice. Think in terms of headlines and sound bites when you Tweet. That's the beauty of it!"

8). Any advice that you would like to share?
"Dip your toe in. See what the water is like! Then jump in and play for a week. It is amazing how many people don't understand the concept of following people. It's the introduction tool of the future. A great technique is to follow the people that follow your followers. The most powerful network tool is to follow a person who has re-Tweeted a person you respect."

9). Your best Twitter experience?
"Finding clients that I never knew before Twitter is the number one. People following my Tweet stream are always good. Becoming interested and looking for solutions using Twitter is a great experience."

10). Top three Tweeps that you would recommend?
@KenBerbury
@ChrisBrogan
@Hotdogladiesman
@bchestnutt
@adrianpitman
@davepeckens
@johnwphilips

11). Other social networks you use regularly?
"I use the Big 3 (Facebook, LinkedIn, and Twitter) along with Motor City Connect and Tumbler about 80% of my social networking time. I'm on over 30 networks in total, but that is my job."

12). What do you think your future with Twitter will be?
"I plan to stay the course. I love where I'm at and where I'm going. I'm hoping that we, the social networking community, can change the mindset of people in this town: spread new ideas and good news and shine a light on what others are doing. Cool brand, cool people, cool ideas. Twitter allows you to spread that information. It has become the most powerful tool for spreading news. I think long and hard before I Tweet negative stuff. If you spread positive vibes people will move in positive direction. Twitter is changing as it becomes more mainstream. There is far more 'cholesterol' in the Twitter stream than before, so it is sometimes hard to find the cool stuff as quickly. But it is still out there.

The Detroit Metro area is in the top 15 media markets in the country, but we are not even in the top 50 in social media. We need to change that. Show your neighbor, your friends, your family. Interest is out there."

Chapter 8 – Other Twitter Software

"The media's power is frail. Without the people's support, it can be shut off with the ease of turning off a light switch."
  - Corazon Aquino

One great power of Twitter is its open structure. It has a great API (*application program interface* in geek language). This means anyone with a good idea and the time to get it done can build a program that can work with Twitter. Here are a few of the hundreds out there that you might want to try.

www.Tweetstats.com

This website is a way to monitor how addicted to Twitter you are becoming. You can also gauge who you talk with the most and your general tone. Great to look at others before you start following them. You can see how much the Tweet, when, and who to.

www.Tweetdeck.com

This is a great way to organize your Twitter life if you have a single Twitter account. It allows you to set up multiple columns that will search for particular items that you are interested in. The only caution is that it is a program rather than a web page. It can slow down your work depending on how much other stuff you have open. But overall, it's worth it!

www.Twellow.com

'*The Twitter Yellow Pages*' is what Twellow declares itself. And that is fairly accurate. If you are looking for something, but not sure where to turn, try Twellow. Caution: Twellow ranks people in categories by the number of followers. Experienced Tweeps will tell you that quality of followers is far more important than quantity, and that it is easy to gain large numbers. However, Twellow is still a useful tool.

http://dossy.org/twitter/karma/

'Twitter karma' allows you to manage your followers and who you are following very effectively. Once you log in, it displays a page that shows you any inequities between your two sets of Tweeps. It then allows you to redress the balance easily.

www.Tweetlater.com

Tweetlater is all about controlling your time when you Tweet. The idea is to automate as many 'monotonous' aspects of Twitter as possible. It is a very feature-rich application and very popular. Caution: do not use automated direct messages 'welcoming' your new followers. If you haven't got the time to welcome them individually, don't bother with the automated reply.

www.Twitpic.com

If you want to post a link to a photograph on Twitter, Twitpic is the tool for you! A very simple website, it allows you to upload photos quickly, and Tweet the link at the click of a single button. It is as simple as Twitter, and is a perfect compliment to it.

The following are a few suggestions from my Tweeps:

ping.fm

ping.fm acts as a social networking hub. It allows you to update Twitter, Facebook, LinkedIn, your blog to name a few all from one place. Recommended by @sandimaki, @alcurtis, @DebraDrummond.

seesmic.com

Another hub application, if you work a lot with Twitter and Facebook, this could help. It also allows you to handle multiple Twitter accounts. Recommended by @DebraDrummond, @Cariann, @davidlingholm

hootsuite.com

If you have multiple Twitter accounts, you should take a look. It combines features of some other applications, and may work well for you. Recommended by @Cariann, @davidlingholm

www.whendidyoujointwitter.com

As simple as it gets, and its name says it all. Enter a Twitter ID, and see when they joined the party! Recommended by @TerryBean, @Cariann

m.slandr.net

An application that improves your Twitter experience for mobile devices. Take a look! Recommended by @davidlingholm.

Case Study 8 – The Final Frontier…?

"I offer a toast. The Undiscovered Country… The future!"
- *Chancellor Gorkon (Star Trek VI: The Undiscovered Country)*

"Hamlet. Act III, scene I."
- *Spock (Star Trek VI: The Undiscovered Country)*

I've been interested in space exploration since the age of seven. But my interest has turned to passion and business over the past three years.

As a result of Twitter, I have met many interesting space-related people. One of the most passionate, creative, and funny is Cariann Higginbotham although that is NOT how I first knew her!

I had begun following the three Space Shuttle orbiters on Twitter. Discovery was about to be launched, and I wished her and the crew well via Twitter. To my surprise, Discovery answered me! We then struck up a conversation… Two weeks later, I logged on to www.SpaceVidCast.com to watch the landing of the Shuttle. Cariann was a moderator on the chat room. She introduced herself to me and told me that she was Discovery! ☺

Hope you get the true sense of Cariann's energy from the case study that follows. If you want to see her (and her hubby), go to www.SpaceVidCast.com every

Thursday night at 10:00 pm EDT, 7:00 pm PDT for their live space show. Something to see!

1). Twitter ID:
@cariann
"I will sometimes moonlight under my personal business name as @spacevidcast or one of the many Twitter accounts that Spacevidcast maintains. These include:

@ISStation
@SSAtlantis, @SSDiscovery, @SSEndeavour
@STS128, @STS129, @STS130

and I think a few others... I'm not totally sure! I also have a viewer or two who also helps out with those accounts, as well as an RSS feed that will send out tweets on those accounts' behalf."

2). Personal or corporate use:
"Well, that's a complicated question! Both? I use @cariann mostly as a personal account... but because we have a small business in Spacevidcast, I will often RT (re-tweet) some of the tweets from @SSDiscovery or @Spacevidcast etc. But that's because I also find it personally interesting.

HOWEVER... @Spacevidcast, which it is a more "corporate" or business account, we don't like to sound too "business-y" on it. We have a very good relationship with our viewers and want to make sure they feel comfortable with us."

3). Did you try anything similar before Twitter?
"LOL! Yes and no. My husband is a confirmed "info-holic" and he has tried just about any and every gadget, app, and OS out there! We dabbled in Dodgeball

for a while... I think we still "Loopt" every once in a while... like when we remember etc. Man, I'm *sure* there are more, I just can't think of any!"

4).   Who introduced you to it?
        "My husband, totally! @bencredible. He was on for a year or two before I really got on board. He is more willing to try whatever is newest and then if I see him sticking with it, I will try it out too. I like to make sure it holds his attention for a while before I get attached!"

5).   When did you start?
        "Huh... I'm not totally sure! I would have to look.... hold on...

        June 11, 2008... WOW! Talk about a late bloomer! (Thanks: http://www.whendidyoujointwitter.com/)

        LOLOLOLOL!!! @bencredible was Feb 22, 2007!"

6).   Why do you use Twitter?
        "Wow... another hard one. Hmmm... well, I like that it keeps me in touch with some people that I don't often get to see. Like my brother who is doing an internship in NY. (I live in MN) It's nice to see what he is up to. But it also has put me in contact with a number of people that I would not normally have met!

        My husband, Ben, and I do this space thing... and we were recently asked to create and talk on a panel about social media in the space industry at the International Space Development Conference '09 in Orlando. I not only got in touch with a ton of people that I had only been following on Twitter, but I got to meet and speak with them on this panel, all thanks to the connections we made on Twitter."

7).   What do you Tweet about?

"Ha! Well, it might be better to ask what I *don't* tweet about. I'll reference who I am with, or who I am meeting... what I am doing... (Although I refuse to simply tweet out that I am eating tuna or having to load the dishwasher!!) But if there is something that I am interested in, like an event... I tweeted about ISDC a LOT! Sometimes you will see silly tweets from me or just stupid things... but I try to keep it positive. I have no need to spread negativity. I think there is enough of that in the world.

On @spacevidcast, there are usually some updates on the latest mission that is going on. But on the @ISStation and @SSAtlantis or @SSEndeavour and @SSDiscovery... those you just have to see to understand. Let's just say they have their own personalities."

8).   Any advice that you would like to share?

"Hmmm.... Yes! I think there have been a lot of critics out there that just look at Twitter and don't really use it, so that makes it harder to understand. You have to give it a try! And, frankly it *won't* be for everyone, but it will be a good fit for *most* people and *most* applications. Heck, if CNN, Ashton Kutcher, Wil Wheaton, me, Zappos, my mother-in-law and the local coffee shop can all find something to talk about, I'm sure you can too.

The hardest part is being sincere. And I know that sounds kinda funny... but I think in general some people have a tendency to just talk for the sake of doing so... and that's not going to attract anyone but spammers.

It's not how many people you follow or are following you... it's the quality of people and connections and conversations that you have that really make Twitter worth while.

LOL! Ben says "And don't be stupid!" I'm not really sure what he means by that... other than the obvious! But he likes what I said too."

9).   Your best Twitter experience?
"WOW. My *best* twitter experience? There are so MANY! I once won a trivia contest and then a prize from @collectSPACE I was re-tweeted by some of my biggest "nerd crushes" @NASA_EDGE and @THE_CO_HOST I've made some really great connections personally and professionally with Twitter... overall it's ALL been a "best" experience. LOL... is that bad?"

10).   Top three Tweeps that you would recommend?
"Oh my... I *have* to say @NASA_EDGE for one. I think @alyankovic is hysterical! And... I think it's a tie between @Yowza and @PostSecret. One saves you money and the other saves lives. Too hard to decide!!

It all just depends on what you like. I like space... so people like @bethbeck, @bnjacobs and @flyingjenny are great for an inside look at things at NASA. @MilesOBrien, @KeithCowing and @jeff_foust are a great look at most things space from an outside kind of view. @glxp and @XPRIZE or @richardbranson are a great look at the private space industry etc. The best thing a new person could do is search. There is http://search.twitter.com/ where you can enter in ANYTHING and find what you are looking for and who is talking about it. It will even look at the latest things that people are talking about (usually called "trending topics"). But you can search for anything. I even searched for just my name once... it came back with some "definition"? From, like the "Tiffany" Dictionary? I don't know, but it was hysterical!"

11).   Other social networks you use regularly?
        "Facebook, Ustream, Skype. That's pretty much my whole arsenal. (And Twitter, of course!)

        The funniest part is that they are all starting to integrate into each other! You can now Twitter or tweet right from the UStream channel you are watching, and if you have your Twitter account linked to your Facebook account, it will update there too!! Ca-razy!"

12).   What do you think your future with Twitter will be?
        "Well... I personally have a very dedicated kind of personality. So, until something "better" comes out and is completely tested by my dear husband... then maybe, but only maybe, will I switch. I like Twitter. I like all of the challenges it poses, with only letting you really get your thoughts out in 140 characters. I like that it is quick. But I also like the flexibility. You can actually link your Twitter account with your RSS reader and then catch up at the end of your day! I mean, how cool is that?!?

Your phone, your computer... your FB [Facebook] account, your UStream account... anywhere and everywhere... or no where. You can turn it off by just texting "off" to your Twitter account at any time. And when you want to turn it back on... you text "on". It could hardly be easier. (Man, I sound like a walking billboard, don't I?) But I wouldn't say it if I didn't mean it.

        LOL... only that I just now realized it's my one year anniversary of being on Twitter! What a great way to celebrate!! Thanks David!"

Part 4 – Who uses Twitter?

"The first step towards getting somewhere is to decide that you are not going to stay where you are."
 - *Unknown Author*

Chapter 9 – Top Twenty Three Tweeps

"A leader is one who knows the way, goes the way, and shows the way."
  - John C. Maxwell

As of May 2009, I'm picking up twenty new followers a day. To people new on Twitter, that may seem a lot, however, other, more seasoned Tweeps might not be impressed with that number. That's OK. But the problem for me is to make a choice from the followers I have. Below is a list of my current favorite twenty three people that I follow, and why! Hopefully, it will show you a few more reasons why and how people use Twitter. The list is in the order that I started following them, or they started following me.

@RyInSpace

My first EVER follower! I had met Ryan at the Mars Society convention in Boulder, Colorado in mid-August, 2008. I have had Twitter conversations with Ryan while he was at the Democratic Convention in Denver in 2008, and while he was at an Avalanche vs. Red Wings game. I think we won! (Go Wings!) ☺ (He is a Penguins fan so Ryan had the last laugh this season!) Ryan is all Canadian, avid hockey fan, going for his PhD, and heading for space! I'll see you up there Ryan ☺.

@BeverlyCornell

Beverly is always bright and cheerful. She is very creative, and 100% dedicated to helping others in her community grow. She loves international business and foreign languages, has a wealth of knowledge on all of these subjects. See Case Study 1 for full details about Beverly! ☺

@ShaunaBizNet

I cannot say enough about dear Shauna (...without greatly increasing the cost of this publication)! Charming and cheerful, talented and technologically astute, she is as smart as she is sharing. Shauna embodies the youthful "anything is possible" attitude of social media in general, and Twitter particularly. See Case Study 2 for more Shauna!

@CharlieCurve

Bacon at its best! Charlie Wollborg is always humorous, as well as insightful. A true Michigan man! Great guy to know. See Case Study 7 to learn more from Charlie.

@TerryBean

Terry is one of the ultimate connectors. He is Charlie's "partner-in-crime" at Motor City Connect, a talented presenter, and very well known in the networking community in Southeast Michigan and beyond. Terry's full story is in Case Study 7.

@dzhu

Danielle (Danling) Zhu has at various times been my inspiration, help desk, mentor, mentee, consultant, boss, officer, support, and always my friend. We first met in the Fall of 2006 at Dearborn Dynamic Toastmasters. Since then, DZ and I have grown our relationship across many facets of life!

@Naim

I met Naim at the first Biznet Tweet-up I attended in November 2008. Because the event was very busy and we did not get to talk very much we learned more by following each other in the weeks after we met. I learned we have many common interests in music, movies, and people we know. He is a very cool guy!

@LaurieSlade

Laurie is a local Michigan personality who I met first through social networking, *and then* in person three times in less than a week. Laurie and I share an interest in all things to do with printing and publishing, and of course social networking!

@DetroitVoice

Larry Henry is a very lively Tweep who is great to talk with on a wide variety of subjects. He can always see a different side to a discussion when needed, and always helps to keep things 'real!' Want to know what's going on around Detroit? Listen to the voice!

@drewie123

Alex was one of the early Tweeps that I got into interesting conversations with. I think our connection originated from our mutual interest in football (the real football that odd parts of the world call *soccer* ☺). Alex lives in Stockholm, Sweden, which is a city I have been lucky enough to visit twice before. Because of that, Alex and I have talked about Sweden too. He is a great connector on Twitter, and is always interesting to read.

@SharneseLaNier

A very kind and caring person, Sharnese always asks if I'm OK when I haven't Tweeted in a few days. Writing a book, running a business, and taking care of family can be a challenge, but it's always nice to know someone cares.

@cletch

It is nice to find someone with a similar Twitter strategy and personality as myself, and Pat Williams has it. Organic growth of followers and following based on Tweets, and never a negative word. Pat has great business and social networking savvy too. I recently discovered something else about Pat: we share the same birthdate (day, month AND year)! How cool is that!

@keithstonehouse

Keith is a great reporter of his business activities. Via Twitter, his enthusiasm for the real-estate business and his community at large shines through. A very dynamic individual and creative in the way he uses Twitter to support his real world activities.

@CantonLibrary

On May 1st, 2008, I gave a speech at Canton Public Library, here in Michigan. At that time, I'd never heard of Twitter. I now follow @CantonLibrary to help keep track of events hosted at the library. This is a very smart and positive way that venues and organizations can keep people informed about what they have to offer. Search for them, and you have an effective calendar right in front of you!

@SSDiscovery

This is a great concept! People can develop strange passions for manufactured objects. I should know. My long suffering wife can tell you of my amazing "pack-rat" abilities. Social networks can take this to another level. THE space shuttle Discovery is the only one I've seen up close and personal back on its launch pad in 1994! Naturally, being the space nerd I am, I started following all three shuttles, plus various NASA missions on Twitter. I've had many delightful conversations with Discovery. She's very pleasant indeed, and is still my favorite shuttle!

@EleART

In January, I put a request out on Twitter to see if anyone was interested in working on a graphic design project with me. About a dozen people responded. Elena was one of them. That project never came about (only my customer knows why), however, we stayed in touch. She is another person that makes their passion for their work and life in general shine through Twitter. Elena also has an artist's view of the world that is amazing to behold. If you want to see her work, take a look at the cover of this book.

@coffeemaverick

David J. Morris is one of a number of Tweeps that I'm looking forward to meeting one day. He is an amazing American success story (follow him, and read his company's web site). David uses Twitter to let his 10,000+ followers know about his ever expanding network of business activities, and also share some of his passions: family, faith, fun, and of course, "The World's Smoothest Coffee".

@DougH

Here is a story of where *real world* and *virtual world* social networking meet. One day, I was traveling down the I-75 freeway in Michigan, heading to a Toastmasters meeting. I was wearing my Toastmasters badge with my name prominently displayed on it. I stopped at the Pilot "Truck Stop" near Monroe to fill up with gas and grab breakfast. In the store, the guy serving me breakfast said, almost cautiously, "Are you related to Bill Haslam?" The answer was "I don't think so". He then proceeded to tell me all about the Haslams and the Pilot Truck Stop empire!

That got me thinking. *I'd never searched for Haslam on Twitter!* When I did the search, the results were amazing! There is a town called Haslam in Texas that a Tweep visited and mentioned. Another Tweep took a picture of the store cat at Haslam's Bookstore in St. Petersburg, FL. And, I came across Doug Haslam. Doug has a great presence on Twitter, along with a great blog. He always has interesting things to say. And an interesting bike to ride! As far as I know, Doug and I are not related. But follow him, and check out his blog anyway!

@LarnacaLad

Let's face it. Most people on the planet have no idea where Cyprus is, let alone Larnaca. However, Richard Horswill is doing a great job of getting it noticed on Twitter. If I need to laugh or brighten the day, I just read Richard's Tweets. You see, Twitter does not have to be all doom and gloom of the 24 hour news variety, or "I'm having my 14th cup of tea today" kind either. It can be just straight out amusing! Find someone who makes you laugh, and follow them!

@ItsDawns

Twitter has a truly global reach and holding conversations with Tweeps at great distances can add new perspective to your daily life. Dawn is probably my most distant Tweep (unless you count @SSDiscovery when she is in orbit! ☺). Dawn is in Perth, Australia. I actually have a number of real life friends in Australia, and that may be why Dawn picked up on me. It is nice to have someone starting a wonderful day as you are ending yours, and Dawn is just that type of positive Tweep that I like!

@AgingBackwards

I started my first serious attempt at a book when I was about 20. At age 31, I had another serious attempt. However, I knew far too little about the process to give it a real chance. 2008 really changed all that. I met people who had the knowledge and drive *to get a book done!* But, in February of 2009 I connected with THE person who enabled EVERYTHING! And that person is Jackie Silver. Jackie and I had been following each other for a few weeks. We spoke for the first time on the phone on February 17th, 2009. I followed her advice. The result is in your hands! To me, this is my greatest success in using Twitter so far. Thank you my friend, thank you!

@LUVMYJP

One day, I mentioned that my Jeep loved the snow in Michigan; I liked it when I would take her out to play in it! Within ten minutes, @LUVMYJP was following me. Curious, I began following back. About ten more minutes went by, and then I saw an RT from @LUVMYJP containing my Tweet. In addition, there were about a dozen other RTs containing the word Jeep... Very curious. Jeep is a very addictive brand with an extremely loyal fan base. It is even worse if you worked at a Jeep production or engineering facility (which I did ☺), and worse still if you ever went off-roading in company vehicles to test them (I did that too!) I confess. I am a Jeep addict! The concept of automatically re-Tweeting ANYTHING to do with Jeeps is a great one for building brand awareness and loyalty. All Jeepsters out there! Sign up! Other brands can learn a lot from this concept too!

The Twitter Workbook team!

These are the people that have helped me with the book that are not mentioned above:

@JustSoMonica

Monica Tombers stepped into the breach and helped me out with a large chunk of proofing and editing towards the end of this book project. Part of my International group, Monica was born in Germany, but came to Michigan as a little girl. Super smart, and extremely creative, Monica gave me plenty of ideas!

@LoriMHarris

A friend, advisor, and mentor, Lori Harris is helping me with the marketing of this book. She has also hatched the idea for the follow-on publication(s), and the need to have you, the reader, register your book to get updates as needed.

@shigj0512

Drita Lulgjuraj can make the darkest and worst situations bearable. We met when we worked together ten years ago and we have been great friends ever since. Exactly 18 months older than me, she moved to Michigan in December 1990 one year after my arrival. However, she is currently back in her birth place of Montenegro through no fault of her own. Her ability to keep laughing and smiling are standing her in good stead. I'm looking forward to welcoming her back to Michigan someday very soon.

Case Study 9 – Moving Marines

"Don't ever give up on something or someone that you can't go a full day without thinking about"
- *Anonymous*

As you get more involved in Twitter, especially in you local area, you might want to attend a Tweet-up. If you are very new to Twitter, it is a great way to jump start things. If you are more experienced, you'll find that these events are a significant way to build your relationships and push them from the virtual world into the real world.

And that is exactly what happened with Debra Drummond and myself. We have been following each other since late 2008. Never having met, I discovered that Debra lived about ten miles away from me and that she is a successful real estate agent. In late April, it was announced through the network that there would be a 'Daveapalooza' to be held on May 22nd. I had not been to a Tweet-up in a while so 'Daveapalooza' sounded great. Since I'm a 'Dave', it was tailor made for me!

At the event I'd just ordered my drink when a tall lady wearing glasses and sporting short blonde hair approached me. Even though we had never met we instantly recognized each other from Twitter. I had to ask Debra her real name. I could not spend the evening calling her "@MichiganMoves". I soon discovered that Debra works in Plymouth (I live in Plymouth) and that she is a Marine Corps veteran. She began to regale me with various impressive Twitter success stories, which led to the interview below! Enjoy!

1).   Twitter ID:
      @MichiganMoves
      @DebraDrummond
      @WomenMarines
      "I began by 'cyber squatting' my @DebraDrummond account. I took the name to stop anyone else but didn't do too much. www.MichiganMoves.com is my website name so it made sense for me to use @MichiganMoves as the first identity I really used. But I then moved my personal and Marine / veteran Tweets to @DebraDrummond and also set up an identity for a veteran's organization I'm involved with called the Women Marines Association. This is @WomenMarines. I now divide my time between the three accounts."

2).   Personal or corporate use:
      "A mixture of both. @MichiganMoves is my main business account and is mostly about real estate. It is still my primary account. @DebraDrummond is mainly personal with some veteran stuff. @WomenMarines is all about veteran and Marine Corps issues. The Women Marines Association is a 501(c)(3) organization supporting women Marines and Marine Corps and veteran issues. I'm the designated social networking person!

      When I setup my primary account, I was Tweeting to much personal information mixed in with the real estate Tweets. Because I setup my second account later, it was difficult to divide my followers between the two. I sent out a Tweet from @MichiganMoves saying that people should follow @DebraDrummond for the veteran Tweets. Some moved to the new account, most did not. And adding the third has made things even worse.

Leveraging my own Tweets can be difficult. I do have a number of people who follow all three accounts. Sending the same Tweet from multiple accounts can be considered SPAM. I guess the followers on all three just have to accept getting two re-Tweets from me occasionally. I don't re-Tweet like that very often. Only if it is critical or urgent and I need to spread the word quickly."

3).   Did you try anything similar before Twitter?
"I signed up for www.ActiveRain.com about three years ago. It is the granddaddy of social networking for agents blogs, connections, questions, and forums. This is what began my journey into social networking! I had foot surgery in December 2007. I used my down time to get more actively involved in ActiveRain and Facebook."

4).   Who introduced you to it?
"A whole combination of things. I read about it on ActiveRain. Don't remember the agent, but a post discussed the advantages of Twitter. Then something very significant happened. I used to live in San Diego, California, and still have family and friends in the area. In October 2007, major wild fires erupted in San Diego. I Googled about the fires. I read that people where sending texts and Tweets because phone lines and the internet system were down in certain areas. That's when I learned the true power of Twitter. Residents were using it to communicate with each other as well as posting first hand accounts of fire activities. I didn't sign up on Twitter until March 2008. And to be honest, *I just didn't get it!* It wasn't until I enrolled in Domus Consulting's social media webinar classes that things took off. I signed up for the

class in September 2008. During the class, they forced everyone to use Twitter. And then, it stuck. I've been loving it ever since!"

5).   When did you start?
"March 2008 signed. [March 7th, 2008 to be exact] I didn't send out many Tweets until September."

6).   Why do you use Twitter?
"It is an interesting transitional tool. As a business and sales person I'm not THAT outgoing. I'm certainly not a natural networker. Twitter allows me to meet people and have a common interest already established. It is far easier to talk to someone new that way. Twitter is a great social facilitator! From an agent's and business perspective, I make connections on line with Twitter, and then take them off line. I was mutually following a woman on Twitter who lived in my home town. We DMed and found we lived two miles apart; we met for coffee, and eventually did business together.

The first Tweet-up I attended was the Southeast Michigan Real Estate Tweet-up organized by @ToddWaller at The Grapevine in Novi, Michigan. This was a monthly meeting just for real estate agents and others in the real estate business. We shared tips, technology and business info. Although we haven't had one since the busy spring market, we still communicate via Twitter and once you've met someone in person, you feel a personal connection to seeing their Tweet.

On the military side, Twitter is great for breaking news that effect vets, fundraisers, charity events, and other time related information. I use it to improve awareness and highlight the role of women in the military."

7).   What do you Tweet about?

"Business: social media articles that I come across, new listings, open houses, photos on Twitpic, and photo blog (including funky things I've found in foreclosed homes!) Also any breaking news I come across; real estate offices closing, a bad traffic accident, a road closed, things like that. Personal: interesting things I hear on the radio, or observe in daily life. Oh, and tennis news. I love tennis! Military: breaking news, bills in congress, troop news from Iraq and Afghanistan, personal interest stories, fundraisers, and other events to reach new members."

8).   Any advice that you would like to share?

"I always tell people start by signing up, send a few Tweets, follow a few people, observe, set up your profile with a photo and a bio so people will follow you back. There's a huge population of real estate agents online sharing lots of great technology info. Read all you can about Twitter. Watch the "In Plain English" video on YouTube or Twitter home page. You never know where your next connection will come from.

And advice for people with or who are planning multiple accounts... Plan ahead! It will simplify things in the long run. I use www.Hootsuite.com and Seesmic Desktop to manage my accounts. It makes life a lot easier!"

9).   Your best Twitter experience?

"Shortly after being at a Tweet-up I saw a Tweet about a class that Missy Caulk (@MissyCaulk) was giving on blogging. Maureen Francis (@MaureenFrancis) sent out a Tweet saying she was going, so I decided to go also. There were about 5-6 of us in the room who showed up because of Twitter! Many of us had never met so it was a great chance to connect and meet the people we had been following, like Karen Moorhead (@A2Karen) at the event.

My other favorite experience is when I shadowed a 5th Grade Teacher for one morning. I Tweeted about going to the school, posted photos of posters I saw, and my reflections afterward on how hard teachers work. Lo and behold, one of my followers had a daughter in one of the classes I observed! Her daughter was STUNNED when her mom brought up my being in the class and that she knew I was there. We both agreed it's because we're moms, *we know everything!*"

10).   Top three Tweeps that you would recommend?
@Swanepoel
@GuyKawasaki
@InfoCentralNAR

11).   Other social networks you use regularly?
"I use Facebook and Twitter mostly. I'm on a lot of others. I sign up for everything. But rarely go on most of them. Ping.fm is essential for posting statuses to all networks at the same time. It makes people think you're everywhere!"

12).   What do you think your future with Twitter will be?
"Social networking and Twitter is the way real estate is moving. In this business, you HAVE to keep up with technology, particularly if you want to work with younger buyers! I came across a quote that I like: 'Agents aren't going away, but agents who are NOT using technology are!' That about sums it up!"

Appendix 1 – Twitter Glossary

"Stand still. The trees ahead and bush beside you are not lost."
- *Albert Einstein*

Some of the new terminology of Twitter along with social networking can be very confusing for a brand new Tweep. Assembled here is a comprehensive listing of terms that you may or may not be familiar with. Only the printed page number of the first occurrence is included.

Word or Phrase	Page	Virtual Social Network	Real World Equivalent
Twitter	vii	The subject of this book!	Something that birds do!
Twitterverse	3	The place where people using Twitter hang out. This is a virtual place that becomes real at Tweet-ups	The universe that contains everything
Tweeps	4	Peeps (people) that you know that use Twitter. (Think P, for people, in TweePs)	Peeps
Tweet	5	A 140 character message sent through Twitter. (Think T, for text, in TweeT)	A message of some sort

Word or Phrase	Page	Virtual Social Network	Real World Equivalent
Facebook	7	A social network used by over 200 million people globally for personal and business communication	Photo album, year book, family album, diary…
Tweet-Up	8	A real world gathering of Tweeps to have real world social interaction	Network event
Blog Weblog	8 15	A web log. Can be used as an online diary, notebook, or journal	Diary, log book
@ symbol (@ElenART)	9	The first character in any individual's Twitter address. To send a Tweet to a Tweep, use a @ in front of their username.	An address
Hash tag (#TTWB)	9	A short label, starting with a # mark, with no spaces used to identify the subject of a Tweet. For example #TTWB is the hash tag for 'The Twitter Workbook'	Label, category
Micro-blog	15	A web log (see above) limited to a small number of characters.	A log entry
YouTube!	16	A social network of user created / supplied video clips	Video library
Tweeple	17	People that you know (or don't know) that use Twitter - Tweeps	People

Word or Phrase	Page	Virtual Social Network	Real World Equivalent
LinkedIn!	21	A social network of professional people around the globe	Business networking association
Re-Tweet, RT	23	Re-sending or forwarding a Tweet from another person	Forwarding a message
Podcast	23	An audio recording that can be downloaded and played on an iPod or similar device.	A recording
Skype	32	A computer based communication tool. Includes voice, video, and chat systems. Service is currently free between Skype users.	Letters, telephone, video recording
MySpace	32	Social networking application similar to Facebook, but less business oriented. See above.	Photo album, year book, family album, diary...
TwitPic	34	A application used with Twitter to store and display photographs.	Photo album
Tumblr, Pandora, Yelp, Vimeo, Flickr	38, 39	Social networking tools	Various stuff...
IRL	45	"In Real Life"	Hmmm... Real life?
LOL	47	Laugh Out Loud (or Lots of love in Britain)	Laughing out loud, or giving lots of love!

Word or Phrase	Page	Virtual Social Network	Real World Equivalent
Ohio	47	A large, mainly flat mid-west state. Home of a great college (Ohio), and great people. Great museums too!!	A place that divides Michigan from the eastern portion of the United States.
Ping.fm	52	Social network tool	A telephone exchange
Ning CollectiveX	54	Social networking tools	Social filing cabinets
DM	57	A Direct Message to another Tweep	A one-on-one conversation
TweetDeck	61	Software designed to work with Twitter.	A bulletin board
Twaddict	62	A Tweep that is addicted to Twitter.	Any other form of addict
SEO	81	Search Engine Optimization. - getting your information on internet search engines.	Marketing technique
BTW	85	'By the way'	By the way…
TwitterFeed, GoogleReader, FriendFeed, TweeterKarma, SocialToo, TwitPic	93	Software to work with Twitter and other social networking tools.	Good stuff
Plaxo	136	Professional social networking web site similar to LinkedIn.	Professional networking group

Appendix 2 – Giving & Receiving

"If you have much, give of your wealth; If you have little, give of your heart."
- *Arab Proverb*

1. Givers

First, the givers, my sponsors for this book. The book could not be produced without them. They are:

- Crestview Technologies, Inc.
- InSights Group
- Tax $aving Solutions, LLC

Details of these three companies follow. Please contact them when you can. You will be pleased that you did! They are excellent to work with.

Crestview Technologies, Inc.

Thank you to the support of the staff at Crestview. Here is their bio and web link:

"Crestview Technologies, Inc. is a Michigan-based information services company. We develop web-based business applications, and deliver web 2.0 integration and consulting services for our enterprise clients.

We bring the best of software development and system integration to our clients. We can supplement in-house application development capability for large clients or serve as the software development department for small clients. Our experienced staff specializes in Microsoft .Net and open source PHP technologies. We build secure, mission-critical web-based business applications for corporations in various industries including financial services, e-commerce and education.

In addition to custom software development, we evaluate and integrate best-of-breed commercial and open source software, especially in the areas of Enterprise 2.0 collaborative software systems."

www.CrestviewTech.com
info@CrestviewTech.com

InSights Group

The InSights Group consists of a great group of people, led by Sandy Maki and Alan Curtis. Bio and website link are below:

"We are here to help you. The InSights Group was formed to help support small businesses. Together, we have created an amazing business center/hub/co-working facility. We are able to bring awesome programs and new and much needed approaches to business through our growing community of positive and amazing individuals. The philosophy we have built this community around is the connection we have to one another. We hope you will become involved and engage with the area's most creative and inspired. Our members are working together to create new ideas, encourage, uplift and inspire one another, and create incredible business growth and prosperity for everyone."

http://www.insights-group.com
sandi@insights-group.com
al@insights-group.com

Tax $aving Solutions

With a wealth of experience and expertise, Karen L. Ryan and her team can do what they say! Thank you for your support Karen! Here is the bio and link:

"Karen L. Ryan has been a Tax Consultant for the past 23 years. She is one of only 35 tax coach all stars in the United States. She received a Bachelor of Science from Indiana University. Through continuing education she has obtained the following credentials and certifications:

- Enrolled Agent, authorized to represent taxpayers in all 50 States.
- Investment Representative (Series 7, 6, 63 and LAH Insurance)
- Certified Senior Advisor
- Real Estate Broker

Karen is a member of the Society of Certified Senior Advisors, The National Association of Tax Professionals, the National Association of Enrolled Agents and the Livingston County Association of Realtors. Karen specializes in tax reduction strategies for small business and the self-employed. Schedule your personal Tax Coach session with Karen today."

www.taxsavingsolutions.com

2. Receivers

It is always important to remember where you came from, where you are, and where you are going to. I have chosen five non-profit organizations that reflect this, and that I believe strongly in. A portion of the profits from the book will be donated to these groups. They and I thank you kindly for the opportunities that this money will provide!

American Cancer Society

In many ways, cancer and its cure have heavily shaped my life, and have constantly welded my English past and American future together. One of my grandmothers died three days before my first business trip to the USA. Since I have been living in the USA my brother, Charles, died shortly before I was to leave on a business trip to Europe. The fight against cancer has helped to cement some life long friendships, and provided spectacular and inspiring events of its own.

Like most families across the world, my own has been tragically effected by the icy grip of cancer. A total of three of my grandparents, and my older brother were all taken by one form or another.

For the last nine years I have been involved in various *Relay For Life* activities. I always contribute in whatever way I can to the cause. This is what has led me to choose The American Cancer Society to receive my ongoing support.

Episcopal Appalachian Ministries

The area of old Lancashire, England, where I was born and raised, was a coal mining area. The badge for my high school featured a block of coal! I had daily reminders of what bad working conditions, poor housing, and low educational expectations could lead too. Some families and fellow students managed to lift themselves out of this circumstance. But all too many did not.

In the US's Appalachia, similar circumstances prevail. A coal "mining" area, living, health, and educational conditions are worsening at an alarming rate. There are an increasing numbers of families suffering for the circumstances of where they live.

I'm a member of St. John's Episcopal Church in Plymouth, Michigan. Each year we send a team down to Appalachia to help families improve their living conditions. Last year, I contributed what I could in terms of money to the effort. This year, I am going to go down and help.

Crossroads of Michigan

Men, women, and children across the globe are homeless and starving everyday. Since the events of 2008, the number has been increasing. Here in Michigan, the situation is becoming critical in some areas. Crossroads helps families in Michigan with food, and gives adults the motivation to improve their circumstances. There are plenty of great stories that come out of simple acts of kindness and sharing. And Crossroads is an inspiring group to be involved with.

Rotary Club of Plymouth a.m.

I have been involved with Rotary International since I was twenty years old, and living in England. After a long break, including a move to Michigan, I was invited to attend a meeting in my town of Plymouth, Michigan. Three projects have touched me deeply:

- *Shelter Box* – a system used to feed and shelter families across the globe afflicted by natural disaster.
- *Tanger School* – a school designed to help children with special needs from the age of three months to six years old.
- *The Miracle League* – providing children of all mental and physical ability the opportunity to play baseball.

At one point in my life I was assessed to see if I should go into a regular school, or a school for special needs. In high school, I was in the Basket Ball club despite having only one fully functional hand. I firmly believe in the best quality education for all, and the opportunity to play any sport that you desire. And always use my personal motto: YES YOU CAN!

The Mars Society

Without sounding too fanciful, the ultimate future of the human race is amongst the stars. If we cannot get there, the human race WILL go the way of the dinosaurs…

The next logical step for humans to visit, settle, and colonize is Mars. Even though the notion seems crazy, 100 years ago, the thought of landing on the moon seemed impossible. And yet, this year is the 40th anniversary of our first landing on that place.

The Mars Society is dedicated to increasing the exploration of the Red Planet, leading to eventual visits by women and men, followed by settlers and colonists.

Technological advancement is ONLY created by expanding human boundaries. And ONLY technological advancement can lead to long term improvement in the quality of life for the general population.

Of my six grandchildren, two have said they want to be astronauts and land on Mars ☺ I would love to see it happen!

Appendix 3 – Your Twitter Tour Guide

"That is the exploration that awaits you! Not mapping stars and nebula, but changing the unknown possibilities of existence."
- *Leonard Nimoy as Cmdr. Spock on Star Trek*

Born and raised in England, David R. Haslam moved to Michigan in November, 1988. He has held a number of technical and marketing positions, including most recently as Publications Manager for the Mopar Division of Chrysler, and as National Business Development Manager for Absolute Data Group. In addition, David has provided management consultation and project management for companies including Ford, Jeep, Disney, Guardian Industries, UNISYS, Norsk Hydro, as well as Chrysler. He has provided training services to the U.S. Navy, General Dynamics IT, General Electric, and Pratt & Whitney Canada.

David has presented keynote addresses and workshops at technical and non-technical conferences. He also presents training and workshop seminars, and regularly speaks to classes and assemblies in the Plymouth-Canton and Wayne-Westland School Districts, ITT Technical Institutes, and Schoolcraft Community College. He has educated students of all ages from Kindergarten to 12th Grade and beyond. His speaking topics range from entertainment to education, and from management and motivation.

David has twice been presented with the *Volunteer In Public Schools* award by the Plymouth-Canton School District. He has an *Advanced Communicator Silver* with Toastmasters International. He is a Rotarian and Director of Marketing for the TEMPO[3] project with The Mars Society.

He has just completed his first book, "The Twitter Workbook" [Yes, this book!]. He is working on his second and third now. David lives in Plymouth, Michigan with his wife, Cecilia, of 20 years, youngest son, two cats, and a small, fat dog.

Contact David at:
drh33@hmsi-inc.com
or
www.twitter.com/davidrhaslam

Started: March 9th, 2009 about 10:00 a.m. EST
Completed: June 15th, 2009 10:35 p.m. EDT

Breinigsville, PA USA ·
30 November 2009

228375BV00004B/38/P